CONCERNING THE NATURE OF THINGS

Six Lectures delivered at the Royal Institution

By

SIR WILLIAM BRAGG

K.B.E., D.Sc., F.R.S

LONDON
G. BELL AND SONS LTD.
1925

PRINTED IN GREAT BRITAIN BY
RICHARD CLAY & SONS, LIMITED,
BUNGAY, SUFFOLK.

PREFACE

It was my endeavour at the Christmas Lectures given at the Royal Institution in 1923-24 to describe certain features of the recent discoveries in physical science. Many of the facts that have come to light might well be the subject of " Lectures adapted to a Juvenile Auditory," and would be at the same time interesting and helpful; interesting because they display a beautiful order in the fundamental arrangement of Nature, and helpful because they have given us light on many old questions, and will surely help us with many that are new. I was aware of two special difficulties. The first was the difficulty of understanding the minuteness of the scale on which the action and properties of the atoms must be represented; but, after all, this was only a difficulty due to unfamiliarity, and would come to a timely end. The other was the difficulty of grasping arrangements in space. There are some who think that this difficulty is incurable, and that it is due to the want of some special capacity, which only a few possess. I am persuaded that this is not the case : we should have nearly as much difficulty in grasping events in two dimensions as in three were it not that we can so easily illustrate our two dimensional thoughts by pencil and paper. If one can turn over a model in one's hand, an idea can be seized in a mere fraction of the time that is required to read about it, and a still smaller fraction of the time that is required to prepare the description. Perhaps some of the readers of this book will be sufficiently interested to make models of the few crystal structures that are mentioned in it, and may even go on to other structures that are described in larger books or in original papers.

I have added somewhat to the lectures as originally given. The additions are intended to make the treatment of the subject a little more complete : they were not very suitable for consideration at the lectures, but are perhaps permissible in the book because the reader can omit them if he desires or read them more than once, or consider them with a model in his hand.

At the end of the book there is a short note on the making of models.

CONTENTS

LECTURE I
THE ATOMS OF WHICH THINGS ARE MADE . . 1

LECTURE II
THE NATURE OF GASES 42

LECTURE III
THE NATURE OF LIQUIDS 83

LECTURE IV
THE NATURE OF CRYSTALS: DIAMOND . . 116

LECTURE V
THE NATURE OF CRYSTALS: ICE AND SNOW . 160

LECTURE VI
THE NATURE OF CRYSTALS: METALS . . . 200

LIST OF PLATES

PLATE		To face page
I.	(A) MODEL OF BISMUTH CRYSTAL. (B) THE SHAKING SAND BOX	17
II.	SHIMIZU-WILSON RAY TRACK APPARATUS	26
III.	ALPHA RAY TRACKS	28
IV.	(A) BAR MAGNETS ON SPIRAL SPRINGS. (B) MODELS OF ATOMS WITH ELECTRONS	32
V.	(A) FLOATING MAGNETS. (B) CRYSTALS IN TUBE CONTAINING EMANATION	38
VI.	(A) TUNING FORK OVER JAR. (B) FOG APPARATUS	56
VII.	CIGARETTE SMOKE	60
VIII.	EXPERIMENT SHOWING THE PRESSURE OF THE ATMOSPHERE	65
IX.	CAVITATION CAUSING EROSION OF PROPELLER BLADES	91
X.	(A) LARGE DROP OF ORTHOTOLUIDINE. (B) ONE SOAP BUBBLE INSIDE ANOTHER	95
XI.	(A) CIRCLES CLEARED BY MINUTE DROPS OF OIL. (B) THE CAMPHOR BOAT	104

LIST OF PLATES

PLATE		To face page
XII.	(A) STORMY WATER. (B) OIL STILLING THE STORM. (C) GRAPE IN SODA WATER	106
XIII.	CRYSTALLINE FORMS	124
XIV.	(A) DIAMOND MODEL. (B) PLANE LATTICE IN THE DESIGN OF A WALL-PAPER	135
XV.	THE CULLINAN DIAMOND	145
XVI.	(A) LAYERS OF THE GRAPHITE CRYSTAL. (B) POSSIBLE FORMS OF THE BENZENE RING	146
XVII.	SNOW CRYSTALS OF VARIOUS FORMS	160
XVIII.	MORE SNOW CRYSTALS	161
XIX.	A HALO AND MOCK SUNS	163
XX.	(A) GLACIER ICE. (B) MODELS OF ICE STRUCTURE	174
XXI.	(A) MODEL OF PENTANE. (B) X-RAY SPECTRUM OF A HYDROCARBON. (C) MODEL OF ROCK SALT	186
XXII.	TWO PHOTOGRAPHS OF ALUMINIUM	202
XXIII.	CRYSTAL GRAINS IN A SAMPLE OF STEEL	202
XXIV.	ILLUSTRATING "CLOSE-PACKING"	204
XXV.	(A) CUBIC PACKING. (B) HEXAGONAL PACKING	206

LIST OF PLATES

PLATE		To face page
XXVI.	THE YIELDING OF ALUMINIUM UNDER STRAIN	211
XXVII.	DAMASCUS BLADES	226
XXVIII.	CEMENTITE CRYSTALS	226
XXIX.	(A) CEMENTITE CRYSTALS BEING BROKEN UP AND ROUNDED OFF. (B) A NEEDLE SCRATCH IN A POLISHED PIECE OF SPECULUM METAL	228
XXX.	EFFECT ON SPECULUM METAL OF RUBBING (WITH FINE EMERY) AND POLISHING (WITH ROUGED LEATHER) . .	228
XXXI.	A CONTINUATION OF PLATE XXX. . .	230
XXXII.	EXPERIMENT SHOWING EFFECT OF TEMPERATURE ON ELECTRICAL RESISTANCE .	230

CONCERNING THE NATURE OF THINGS

LECTURE I

The Atoms of which Things are Made.

NEARLY two thousand years ago, Lucretius, the famous Latin poet, wrote his treatise *De rerum natura*—concerning the nature of things. He maintained the view that air and earth and water and everything else were composed of innumerable small bodies or corpuscles, individually too small to be seen, and all in rapid motion. He tried to show that these suppositions were enough to explain the properties of material things. He was not himself the originator of all the ideas which he set forth in his poem; he was the writer who would explain the views which were held by a certain school, and which he himself believed to be true. There was a rival set of views, according to which, however closely things were looked into, there would be no evidence of structure : however the water in a bowl, let us say, was subdivided into drops and then again into smaller drops and so on and on, the minutest portion would still be like the original bowl of water in all its properties. On the view of Lucretius, if subdivision were carried out sufficiently, one would come at last to the individual corpuscles or *atoms :* the word atom being taken in its original sense, something which *cannot be cut.*

There is a mighty difference between the two views. On the one, there is nothing to be gained by looking into the structure of substances more closely, for however far we go we come to nothing new. On the other view, the nature of things as we know them will depend on the properties of these atoms of which they are composed, and it will be very interesting and important to find out, if we can, what the atoms are like. The latter view turns out to be far nearer the truth than the former; and for that all may be grateful who love to enquire into the ways of Nature.

Lucretius had no conception, however, of atomic theories as they stand now. He did not realise that the atoms can be divided into so many different kinds, and that all the atoms of one kind

ATOMS OF WHICH THINGS ARE MADE 3

are alike. That idea is comparatively new: it was explained with great clearness by John Dalton at the beginning of the nineteenth century. It has rendered possible the great advances that chemistry has made in modern times and all the other sciences which depend on chemistry in any degree. It is easy to see why the newer idea has made everything so much simpler. It is because we have to deal with a limited number of sorts only, not with a vast number of different individuals. We should be in despair if we were compelled to study a multitude of different atoms in the composition of a piece of copper, let us say; but when we discover that there is only one kind of atom in a piece of pure copper, and in the whole world not many different kinds, we may feel full of enthusiasm and hope in pressing forward to the study of their properties, and of the laws of their combinations. For, of course, it is in their combinations that their importance lies. The atoms may be compared to the letters of the alphabet, which can be put together into innumerable ways to form words. So the atoms are combined in equal variety to form what are called molecules. We may even push the analogy a little further and say that the association of words into sentences and passages conveying meanings of every kind is like the combination of molecules of all kinds and in all proportions to form structures and materials that have an infinite variety of appearances and properties and can carry what we speak of as life.

The atomic theory of Lucretius did not contain, therefore, the essential idea which was necessary for further growth and progress. It withered away, and the very atom came to be used in a vague incorrect fashion as meaning merely something very small: as sometimes in Shakespeare's plays, for instance. In another and very different application of " atomic " theory Lucretius was strangely successful. He had the idea that disease was disseminated by minute particles. At the time of the Renaissance Fracastoro was inspired by the atomic theory of infection as he read it in the poem of Lucretius; but after his day the secret of bacteriology was again covered up until it was laid bare by Pasteur.[1]

Let us think of Nature as a builder, making all that we see out of atoms of a limited number of kinds; just as the builder of a house constructs it out of so many different kinds of things—bricks, slates, planks, panes of glass, and so on. There

---

[1] See " The Legacy of Rome " (Oxford University Press), p. 270—an article by Dr. Singer.

ATOMS OF WHICH THINGS ARE MADE

are only about ninety sorts of atoms, and of these a considerable number are only used occasionally. It is very wonderful that all the things in the world and in the universe, as far as we know it, are made of so few elements. The universe is so rich in its variety, the earth and all that rests on it and grows on it, the waters of the seas, the air and the clouds, all living things that move in earth or sea or air, our bodies and every different part of our bodies, the sun and moon and the stars, every single thing is made up of these few kinds of atoms. Yes, one might say, that is so: but if the builder is given bricks and mortar and iron girders he will build you an infinite variety of buildings, palaces or cottages or bridges; why may not Nature do something like that? But one has to think that when a builder sets out to make a structure he has a plan which has cost thought to devise, and he gives instructions to his workmen who are to carry out his wishes, and so the structure grows. We see him walking about with his plans in his hand. But the plans of the structures of Nature are locked up in the atoms themselves. They are full of wonder and mystery, because from them alone and from what they contain grows the infinite variety of the world. How they came to be such treasure-houses we are not asking now. We ask ourselves what these atoms are like: we have been asking the question ever since their exceeding importance began to be realised more than a hundred years ago. Have they size and form and other characteristics such as are possessed by bodies with which we are familiar? We must look into these points.

But first let us realise that in the last twenty-five years or so we have been given, so to speak, new eyes. The discoveries of radioactivity and of X-rays have changed the whole situation: which is indeed the reason for the choice of the subject of these lectures. We can now understand so many things that were dim before; and we see a wonderful new world opening out before us, waiting to be explored. I do not think it is very difficult to reach it or to walk about in it. In fact, the new knowledge, like all sudden revelations of the truth, lights up the ground over which we have been travelling and makes things easy that were difficult before. It is true that the new lines of advance now open lead the way to fresh difficulties: but therein lies the whole interest and spirit of research. We will try to take the first steps into the new country so that we may share in the knowledge that has already come, and comes in faster every day.

ATOMS OF WHICH THINGS ARE MADE

We go back to our questions about the atoms. Before the new period set in remarkably accurate answers had already been given to some of them, at least. In this theatre of the Royal Institution, Lord Kelvin gave several addresses which dealt with the properties of atoms, and especially with their sizes. By several most ingenious and indirect devices he arrived at conclusions which we are now able to test by accurate methods; and we find that he was remarkably close to the truth. It was, of course, far more difficult to say what was the size of any particular atom than it was to say how much larger one atom was than another. For instance, the sizes of the atoms of potassium and carbon could be roughly compared by taking into account the relative weights of equal volumes of the solid potassium metal and of diamond which is a form of pure carbon. Potassium is lighter than water, the diamond is three and a half times as heavy. We know from chemical observations that the individual potassium atom is rather more than three times as heavy as the carbon atom. If we suppose that the packing of the atoms in the two cases is the same (as a matter of fact, we now know that it is only approximately so) we must conclude that the atoms in the metal potassium are much larger than the carbon atoms in the diamond, because, though heavier individually, they pack so as to make a lighter material.

To make a reasonable estimate of the actual size of any one atom is a much more difficult matter, but all the four lines of reasoning which Kelvin employed led him to very nearly the same result. "The atoms or molecules of ordinary matter must be something like the 1/10,000,000th or from the 1/10,000,000th to the 1/100,000,000th of a centimetre in diameter."[1] Our new methods tell us that the diameter of the carbon atom in diamond is 1·54 hundred millionths of a centimetre and that of the atom in the metal potassium is 4·50 hundred millionths. We see that Lord Kelvin's estimate was wonderfully near the truth, considering the indirect and inexact methods which alone were at his disposal.

In Fig. 1 are shown sections of certain atoms on a scale of fifty millions to one. The inserted figures give in each case the distance, in hundred-millionths of a centimetre, between the centres of two neighbouring atoms in the pure substance. For example, the distance between two carbon atoms in the diamond is 1·54 hundred-millionths of a centimetre. In the case of oxygen the

[1] From a Friday Evening Discourse before the Royal Institution of Great Britain, March 4th, 1881.

ATOMS OF WHICH THINGS ARE MADE

diameter has been calculated from the structure of crystals in which oxygen occurs. If the lecture-room of the Royal Institution were magnified as much as the atoms of Fig. 1, its height would be greater than the distance from the earth to the moon. We need some such com-

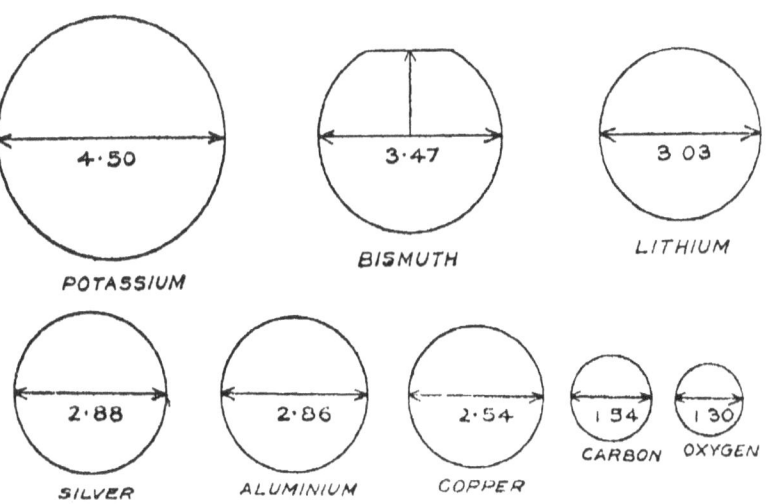

FIG. 1.—Sections of some common atoms, in hundred-millionths of a centimetre. In reference to bismuth see below (p. 12) and Plate I A.

parison as this to make us realise the excessive smallness of the things of which we are talking. At the same time, we must keep in mind that they are not negligible because they are small: they are the actual elements of construction of the world and of the universe, and their size has nothing to do with their importance. But their smallness accounts readily for the ease with which we all overlook them, and for the difficulty we have in examining them when at last we have realised what they mean to us. The value of the new methods of which I propose to speak lies in the fact that they enable us to deal with them although they are so small.

We have now answered in a way the question as to the size of the atoms; but when we go further and ask ourselves about the shape we are not so successful.

The chemist, whose science is immediately concerned with the combinations of atoms, has rarely found it necessary to discuss their shapes, and gives them no particular forms in his diagrams. That does not mean that the shapes are unimportant, but rather that the older methods could not define them. There is one sense, however, in which the chemist pays much attention to form. The atoms in a compound are arranged in some fashion or other which is important to the combination. If one could see it and sketch it, one would be obliged to show it in perspective. In the science of organic chemistry especially it is found to be necessary to imagine such arrangements in space. It is not enough to represent them on the flat with no perspective at all; in fact, it is obvious that any flat design must be

ATOMS OF WHICH THINGS ARE MADE 11

imperfect in any sort of chemical picture. We are unfortunately compelled to use the flat for our drawings; solid models in space are costly to make, while paper and pencil are cheap. It is curious to reflect what a handicap this technical difficulty puts on the proper development of a very important matter. Now, when we come to prescribe the arrangements of the atom to its neighbours, and to say that if one neighbour lies in this direction, another must lie in that, we are, in effect, giving shape to our atoms; at any rate, it is all the shaping that can be done for the present. We cannot do more until we know more about the internal structure of the atom: what its parts are, and how they are disposed to one another.

In the newer work, as we shall see, the arrangement of the atoms is much more closely examined, and for the first time their actual distances apart are measured. We find it absolutely necessary to make models because we do not see with sufficient clearness if we are content to draw on paper. We represent our atoms as round balls, and we find that we are able to represent most of our discoveries in this way. This really means that when an atom has several neighbours of the same kind it is equally distant from them all; and this is actually the case. Nevertheless, there are exceptions, as in the crystal of pure bismuth, where each atom has six neighbours and three of them are closer than the other three. We have to make a ball with three flats on it for use in constructing the bismuth model (Plate I A).

Let us now ask ourselves what binds the atoms together into the various combinations and structures. Like our builder, we have got in our materials—the bricks, slates, beams and so on; we have our various kinds of atoms. If we look round for mortar and nails we find we have none. Nature does not allow the use of any new material as a cement. The atoms cling together of themselves. The chemist tells us that they must be presented to one another under proper conditions, some of which are very odd; but the combination does take place, and there is something in the atoms themselves which maintains it when the conditions are satisfied. The whole of chemistry is concerned with the nature of these conditions and their results.

The atoms seem to cling to one another in some such way as two magnets do when opposite poles are presented to each other; or two charges of electricity of opposite nature. In fact, there is no doubt that both magnetic and electric

ATOMS OF WHICH THINGS ARE MADE 13

attractions are at work. We are not entirely ignorant of their mode of action, but we know much more about the rules of combination—that is to say, about the facts of chemistry—than we do about the details of the attractions. However, we need not trouble ourselves about these matters for the present; we have merely to realise that there are forces drawing atoms together.

We may now ask why, if there are such forces, the atoms do not all join together into one solid mass? Why are there any gases or even liquids? How is it that there are any atoms at all which do not link up with their neighbours? What prevents the earth from falling into the sun and the final solidification of the entire universe?

The earth does not fall into the sun because it is in motion round the sun, or, to be more correct, because the two bodies are moving round one another. It is motion that keeps them apart; and when we look closely into the matter we find that motion plays a part of first importance in all that we see, because it sets itself against the binding forces that would join atoms together in one lump. In a gas, motion has the upper hand; the atoms are moving so fast that they have no time to enter into any sort of combination with each other: occasionally atom must meet atom and, so to speak, each hold out vain hands to the other, but the pace is too great and, in a moment, they are far away from each other again. Even in a liquid where there is more combination and atoms are in contact with each other all the time, the motion is so great that no junction is permanent.

In a solid the relative importance of the attractive forces and the motion undergoes another change: the former now holds sway, so that the atoms and the molecules are locked in their places. Even in the solid, however, the atoms are never perfectly still; at the least they vibrate and quiver about average positions, just as the parts of an iron bridge quiver when a train goes over it. It is difficult to realise that the atoms and molecules of substances which appear to be perfectly at rest, the table, a piece of paper, the water in a glass, are all in motion. Yet many of the older philosophers grasped the fact. For example, Hooke, an English physicist of the seventeenth century, explains by a clear analogy the difference which he supposed to exist between the solid and the liquid form: ascribing it to a movement of the atoms which was greater in the liquid than in the solid state. " First," he says, " what is

ATOMS OF WHICH THINGS ARE MADE 15

the cause of fluidness? This I conceive to be nothing else but a very brisk and vehement agitation of the parts of a body (as I have elsewhere made probable); the parts of a body are thereby made so loose from one another that they easily move any way, and become fluid. That I may explain this a little by a gross similitude, let us suppose a dish of sand set upon some body that is very much agitated, and shaken with some quick and strong vibrating motion, as on a millstone turn'd round upon the under stone very violently whilst it is empty; or on a very stiff drum-head, which is vehemently or very nimbly beaten with the drumsticks. By this means the sand in the dish, which before lay like a dull and unactive body, becomes a perfect fluid; and ye can no sooner make a hole in it with your finger, but it is immediately filled up again, and the upper surface of it levelled. Nor can ye bury a light body, as a piece of cork under it, but it presently emerges or swims as 'twere on the top; nor can ye lay a heavier on the top of it, as a piece of lead, but it is immediately buried in sand, and (as 'twere) sinks to the bottom. Nor can ye make a hole in the side of the dish, but the sand shall run out of it to a level. Not an obvious property of a fluid body, as such, but this does imitate; and all this merely caused by the vehement agitation of the conteining vessel; for by this means, each sand becomes to have a vibrative or dancing motion, so as no other heavier body can rest on it, unless sustein'd by some other on either side : nor will it suffer any body to be beneath it, unless it be a heavier than itself."

Hooke's experiment can be repeated in a somewhat different form. A cylindrical metal box, ten inches wide and three inches deep, is fixed upon a platform which is supported on metal balls so that it moves easily. It is connected through an eccentric joint with a turning table as shown in Plate I B. When the wheel is turned rapidly, the box and the sand which it contains are violently agitated as Hooke prescribes. The details of the mechanism are best understood by reference to the figure. A heavy metal ball placed on top of the sand disappears at once, and light objects, such as ping-pong balls, rise to the surface. A very ludicrous effect is produced if we bury in the sand some of the celluloid figures which cannot be made to lie down because they are heavily weighted at the bottom. The figures slowly rise out of the sand and finally stand erect. (Plate I B and Fig. I A.)

ATOMS OF WHICH THINGS ARE MADE 17

We know now that the motion of the atoms of a body is really its heat: that the faster they move or vibrate the hotter the body becomes. Whenever we warm our hands by the fire, we allow the energy radiated by the fire to quicken up the movements of the atoms of which the hands are composed. When we cool any substance we check those movements. If we could still them

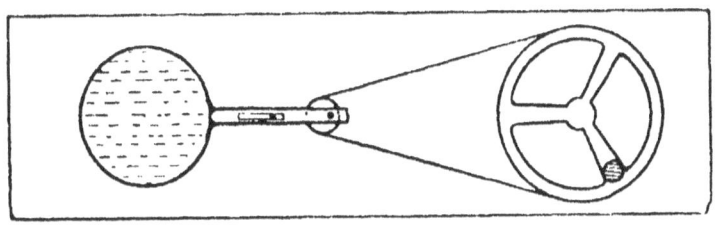

FIG. 1, A.

altogether we should lower the temperature to a point beyond which it would be impossible to go, the absolute zero, as it is usually called, 273 degrees centigrade below zero.

As I have said already, we have found two new allies, radioactivity and X-rays, in our attempt to see the very minute atom. They have increased the fineness of our vision some ten thousand times. The microscope had done its best for us; but the smallest thing which it could show us was composed of billions of atoms. No improvement could be made in the microscope lenses: technique had reached its highest. The difficulty was really due to the fact that light is a wave motion and light waves cannot show us the details of objects unless the objects are much larger in every way than the length of the wave. We wanted a new light of very short wave length. It came in the form of the X-rays. At the same time radioactivity came to show us what a single atom could do by itself if it were given a tremendous speed. We can now both see the single atom, indirectly no doubt but quite usefully, and also observe something which it does: the X-rays help us with the former and radioactivity with the latter. I hope to explain to you how both these agents are adding to our knowledge, and I will take radioactivity first.

The atom of radium might be roughly represented in size by one of the larger balls that lie before you. It is one of the heaviest and largest of the atoms; a number of them together form a substance which is a metal like iron or gold. It is, of itself, in no obvious way peculiar as long as it continues to be an atom of radium, but, for some reason, which no one understands, there comes a moment when it bursts. A small portion is hurled away like the shot from a gun, and the remainder recoils like the gun itself. The remainder is not radium any more, it is a smaller

ATOMS OF WHICH THINGS ARE MADE

atom, having entirely different properties. The radium has turned into a new substance. As a matter of fact, the new substance is a gas, while the projectile turns out to be an atom whose weight is low down in the series of atomic weights, the lowest but one in fact; it is called helium. No one knows what brings about the explosion, nor does any one know a way of hastening it, or of hindering it. The radium atom is just as likely to explode at any given moment if it is in a furnace as if it is immersed in liquid air. Indeed, its independence of its surroundings in respect to its time of explosion is shown in a much stronger light by the fact that combination with other atoms makes no change. Combination, or molecule-forming, is, no doubt, concerned with the outside arrangements of the atoms, but the bursting of the atom comes from inside.

The old alchemist tried to find a means of converting one atom into another, preferably lead into gold. In the action of radium there is a transmutation, to use an old word, of the kind of which the alchemist dreamt. But it is not exactly what he strove for, in two ways. In the first place, it cannot be controlled by human will —which is extraordinary, because there are not so many things of which this can be said. Even when an operation is quite beyond our power to understand, we can often decide whether or no it shall happen. We cannot understand how a seed germinates, much less make one that will do so; but we can lock up seeds in a drawer and prevent them from germinating as long as we like. But the radium explosion does not wait on anything which we do.

In the second place, the transmutation does not end in gold: it ends rather in lead. The gas which consists of atoms of radium that have shot off one atom of helium is very short-lived: the average life of each of its atoms is a little less than four days, in contrast to the average life of the radium atom, which is about two thousand years. The second explosion " transmutes " the gas atom into a new substance called Radium A, and on the occasion another helium atom is shot away. There is a further succession of explosions, at very varying average intervals, and the final product is actually lead, not gold. The gas was called the " radium emanation " by Rutherford, who discovered it.

The whole operation is very wonderful, but I want to call attention to what happens to the projectile when it has left the gun. The velocity with which it starts is so great that one could

ATOMS OF WHICH THINGS ARE MADE 21

never have thought any particle of matter could have possessed it. When Huyghens argued with Newton on the subject of the nature of light, he condemned Newton's idea that light consisted of a flight of corpuscles, on the ground that material particles could not possibly travel as fast as light had just been found to move. It is curious that we now find atoms moving with speeds comparable with, a tenth or twentieth of, that which then seemed impossible. There are even certain particles, called electrons, also emitted by radioactive substances, which travel, in some cases, very nearly as fast as light. It is also curious that the second argument of Huyghens was equally unfortunate in view of the observed phenomena of radioactivity. He said that it would be impossible, on Newton's theory, for two people to look into each other's eyes because the particles would meet each other and fall to the ground. We shall presently see that this argument also is set at nought by the facts of radioactivity.

The velocity with which the helium atom begins its flight is something like 10,000 miles in a second. In less than a minute it could get to the moon and back again if the speed were maintained, but the curious thing is that for all the speed and energy with which it starts it never gets far when it has to pass through anything material. Even if it is allowed to finish its course in the air, its speed has fallen to something of quite ordinary value after it has traversed a course of two or three inches in length. The course is, in general, perfectly straight, as we shall presently see in an actual experiment, and this is the very important point which we must consider with particular care. At first sight one does not realise how remarkable it is that its path should be *straight :* one thinks of a bullet fired through a block of wood, let us say, and making a cylindrical hole, or of the bullet in its straight course through the air. But the comparison is unfair. The bullet is a mass of lead enormously heavier than any molecule which it meets, and it brushes the air aside. But the helium atom is lighter and smaller than the atoms of nitrogen or oxygen of which the atmosphere is mainly composed, and we must think of some more truthful comparison. Suppose that a number of billiard balls are lying on a billiard table, and let them represent air molecules. If they are in movement the picture will be more correct, but the point does not really matter. Now let us drive a ball across the table aiming at a point on the opposite cushion, and watch what happens as the ball tries to get through the crowd that lies on the table, which crowd may or may not be in movement. It hits one of the balls and is turned to one side; it hits several in succession, and soon loses all trace of its original direction of movement. Shall we now drive it with all the force we can, and see whether it keeps any more nearly to the straight path? We try, and find that there is no improvement at all. The straight path cannot be obtained by any increase of speed, however great.

This picture or model is much more faithful than that of the moving bullet, and shows more clearly the remarkable nature of the radium effect. A helium atom must encounter a very large number of air molecules if it proceeds on a straight-line path, and if the atoms are of the size we have supposed them to be. In fact, the molecules lie far more thickly on the path than we can represent by the billiard-table model. It is possible to calculate how many air molecules, some oxygen, some nitrogen, would be pierced by a straight line three inches long drawn suddenly at any moment in the air, and the result is to be expressed in hundreds of thousands. How can the helium atom charge straight through this crowd, every member of which is heavier than itself? It does so, however, and we have to find some explanation.

Perhaps it might be thought that the straightness of the path is only apparent, and that if we could look into it in sufficient detail we should see that it was made up of innumerable zigzags made in going round the molecules met with. But a moment's reflection shows that the idea is absurd: the atom would need to possess the intelligence of a living being to give it the power of recovering a line once lost. If there were a cake shop on the opposite side of a crowded street, and if we gave a boy sixpence and directed him to the shop, he would no doubt pursue a path which was effectively straight, though it would be broken up by the need of dodging the various people and vehicles which the boy met with. But one cannot imagine an atom of helium doing anything of the sort.

There is only one way of explaining the marvel of the straight path: we must suppose that the helium atom *goes through* the molecules it meets, and that somehow it is enabled to do so by the fact that it is moving at such an unusual speed. It is a very startling idea. However, no other suggests itself; and, as a matter of fact, it turns

ATOMS OF WHICH THINGS ARE MADE

out that we can explain many other things by its aid. Consequently, we feel sure that we are on the right track.

It is time now that we should see this effect with our own eyes: the conclusion at which we have arrived is so new and so full of meaning that we would like to have an experimental demonstration if possible, and convince ourselves of the reality of these straight-line paths. We owe to Mr. C. T. R. Wilson a beautiful piece of apparatus which gives us a vivid picture of what happens, and we will make use of it at once. The experiment is, in my opinion, one of the most wonderful in the world of science. We are going to see the actual tracks of separate helium atoms, each of which begins its course at a speed of ten thousand miles a second and yet completes it after traversing about three inches of air. But

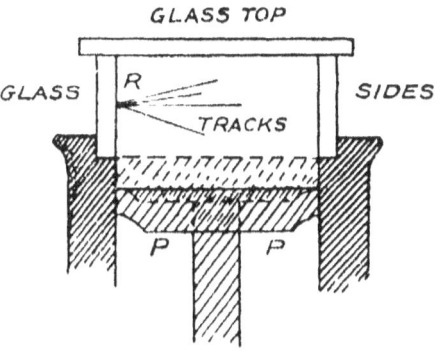

FIG. 2.—Section of the expansion chamber in Mr C. T. R. Wilson's apparatus for measuring the track of helium atoms (see also Plate II).

The piston *PP* is dropped suddenly from the position indicated by the dotted lines to the position indicated by the full lines: so that the air in the chamber is suddenly chilled by expansion and fog settles on the tracks of the helium atoms shot out by the radium at *R*.

we must first enter upon some explanation of how the apparatus works; for there are ingenious devices in it.

There is a cylindrical box of brass, with a glass top and a base which can be raised or lowered so as to alter the depth of the box. There is a machinery of wheels, cranks and levers by which the bottom of the box can be suddenly dropped at convenient intervals. Whenever this happens, the air or other gas which the box contains is chilled by the sudden expansion. We shall study effects of this kind more carefully in the next lecture. At the side of the box, in its interior, a minute speck of radium is mounted on a suitable holder. Every moment some of its atoms break up and expel atoms of helium, of which a certain number are shot straight into the box. The diameter of the box is big enough to allow the atoms to finish their courses in the air within. The average life of radium is so long that even if the apparatus held together for two thousand years, half of the radium speck would still be left. Yet each second, ten, twenty or a hundred atoms disappear in the expulsion of the helium atoms. Perhaps in no better way can it be shown how many atoms are concentrated in a small compass.

The air in the chamber is kept damp, con-

PLATE II.

[*By courtesy of the Cambridge Scientific Instrument Co.*]

Shimizu-Wilson ray track apparatus.

The apparatus which shows the tracks of the helium atom shot out by radium. The chamber as sketched in Fig. 2 is to be seen on the upper left of the figure. The disc to the left of it is a screen, in which is a hole. The light from a lantern—not shown—shines through the hole and lights up the fog tracks. A second screen revolves, and lets the radium rays, i.e. the helium atom, shine into the chamber just before the expansion is made. On the right is the driving machinery.

sequently the chill due to expansion tends to produce a fog. Fog when it has to settle prefers to deposit itself on a solid nucleus of some sort, rather than to form independent drops in the air. The small particles of dust, if there are any, are made use of, which is the reason why fogs so readily form in a dirty atmosphere. But of all things moisture prefers to settle on those atoms through which the helium atom has passed. The reason is that the atom is temporarily damaged by the transit: a small portion has generally been chipped away. The portion removed is what we now call an "electron"; it is charged with negative electricity, and the atom which has lost it is correspondingly charged with positive electricity. The electron set free settles on some neighbouring atom, sooner or later; and in consequence there are two charged atoms, one positive and one negative, where previously there were no charged atoms at all. The charged atoms have a great attraction for moisture, and the fog forms on them in preference to anything else. If, therefore, a helium atom has just made its straight road through the gas, and has left behind it numbers of charged atoms on its track, and if, at that moment, the sudden expansion causes a chill, fog settles along the track. A bright light is made to illuminate the chamber, so that the fog tracks are visible as bright straight lines, showing against the blackened background of the bottom of the cylindrical chamber. They last a few seconds, and then the fog particles slowly disperse. If the helium atom completes its track just before the fog is formed, the line is sharp and clear; because the charged atoms have not had time to wander from the track. But if the track is made some time before the expansion, the line of fog is more diffuse. It is to be remembered that the helium atoms are being shot out all the time, day and night; but it is only when an expansion is made that tracks are made visible.[1]

If we watch the successive expansions, we see that the tracks, though quite straight over large parts of their course, do undergo at times sudden sharp deflection, especially when they are nearing the end. This remarkable effect turns out to be most important, and we must refer to it presently.

Let us now try to picture to ourselves in what way we must modify our first conception of the atom so that we can explain the effects we now

[1] In the lecture the working of the apparatus was illustrated by a kinematograph film which had been made for the purpose. It showed a series of successive expansions, each forming a new set of lines like those shown in Plate III.

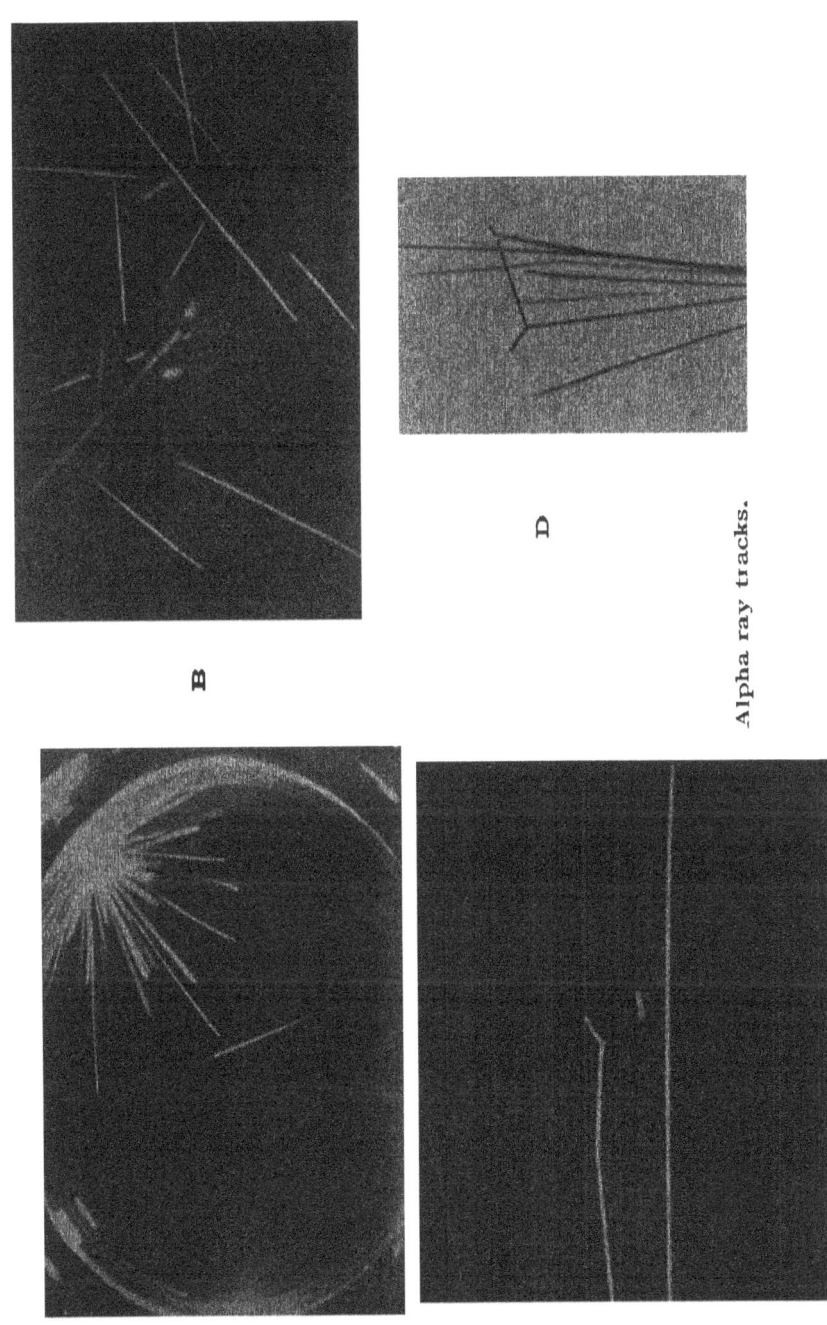

Alpha ray tracks.

see. The atoms must be so constituted that when they meet one another in the ordinary way, as, for example, when molecules of oxygen collide in the atmosphere, they behave as if each had a domain of its own into which no other might enter. Or, when they are pressed together, as in a solid, they occupy as a whole an amount of space which is sufficient to make room for them all. But when one atom—the helium atom is our chief example—is hurled against others with sufficient speed, the one atom goes through the other, as if the defences round the domains had been broken down. We find a satisfactory explanation when we imagine each atom to be like a solar system in miniature. There is to be a nucleus, corresponding to the sun, and round the nucleus there are to be satellites or planets, which we call electrons. The nucleus is charged with positive electricity; each electron is charged with negative electricity, and all electrons are alike. The positive charge on the nucleus is just enough to balance the united negative charges of the electrons. The electrons are supposed to be in movement, just as the planets are revolving round the sun, but the movements are no doubt complicated, and their nature need not for the moment concern us at all.

Instead, therefore, of a round hard ball of a certain size, which was our first rough picture of an atom, we have something like a solar system in miniature. We can at once see how one atom of this kind can pass through another, just as we might imagine one solar system passing through another, without injury to either provided that no one body of one system made a direct hit on a body of the other and that the motion was quick enough. The latter condition is necessary because if one solar system stayed too long inside or in the neighbourhood of another there would certainly be very serious disturbances of the courses of the planets.

But then, we may ask, how can an atom, if this be its nature, have the power of keeping another outside its own domain? How can it appropriate any portion of space to itself, and prevent the intrusion of another atom when the speed at which they meet is low? The explanation becomes clear when we consider the special arrangement of the positive and negative charges. Every atom is surrounded by a shell or cloak of electrons; and, when two atoms collide, it is their shells which first come close together. Since like charges of electricity repel one another, the two atoms will experience a force which tends to keep them apart:

ATOMS OF WHICH THINGS ARE MADE

in other words, they will resist encroachment on their own domains. This is, no doubt, a very rough picture of what actually happens, and as a matter of fact it is difficult to explain the strength of the resisting forces on such a simple hypothesis. Still, it is on the right lines, no doubt. When the two atoms approach each other at a high speed, the system of electrons and nucleus of one atom slip through those of the other. A model will help to illustrate the point.

Plate IV A shows a set of bar magnets mounted on spiral springs and standing erect. The top of the inside magnet is a north pole, and the tops of the magnets of the outside ring are south poles. The model represents roughly the central nucleus surrounded by a ring of electrons. In the model everything is in one plane; in the atom it is not so, but the point is not important. A single magnet is suspended by a long thread from a point vertically over the " nucleus " magnet. Its lower end is a south pole and the length of the thread is such that the swinging magnet just clears the fixed magnets. Observe now that if we pull the swinging magnet to one side (S in Fig. 3, a), but not too far, it moves towards the fixed set and is unable to enter in. It seems to knock at the door at one place after another, but always recoils. Just so would an electron beat in vain against the outer defences of an atom, if it did not beat hard enough. We can easily imagine that if the single swinging magnet were replaced by a system of magnets, like our

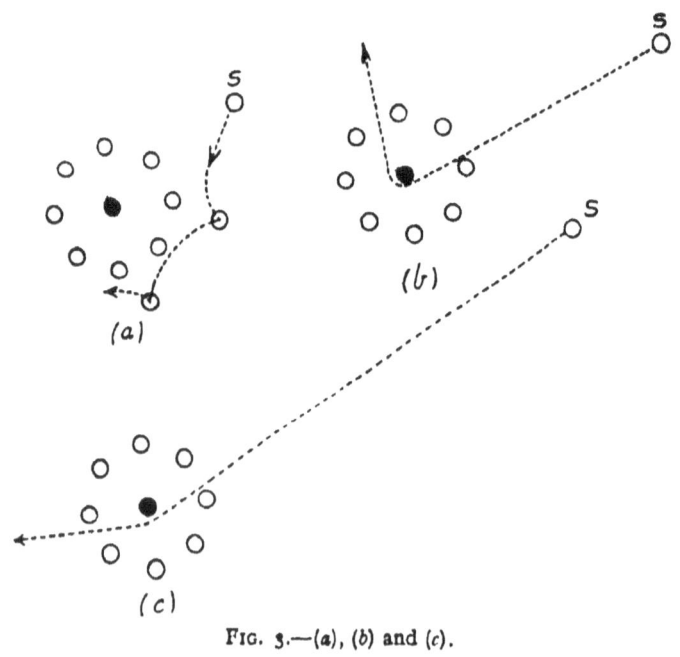

FIG. 3.—(a), (b) and (c).

stationary set, the same result would follow. Here we have a picture representing our atoms, as we now think of them, beating against each other and recoiling; each occupies a certain domain of space and prevents the intrusion of any other atom.

But if the swinging magnet is drawn sufficiently

PLATE IV.

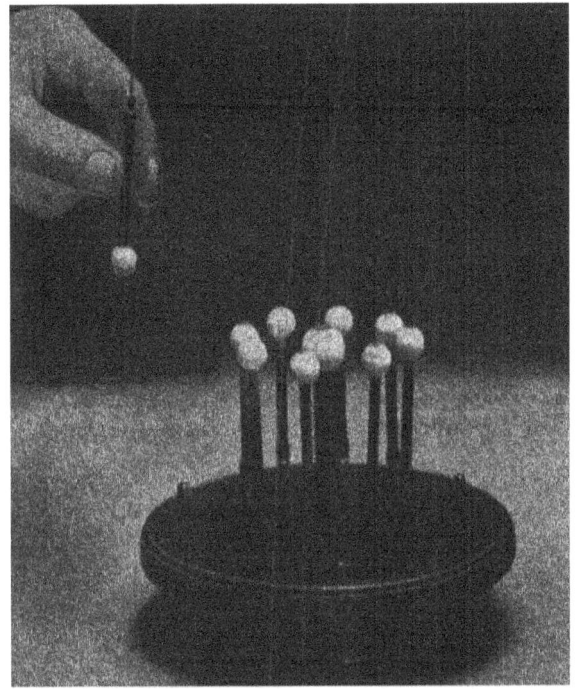

A. Bar magnets on spiral springs.

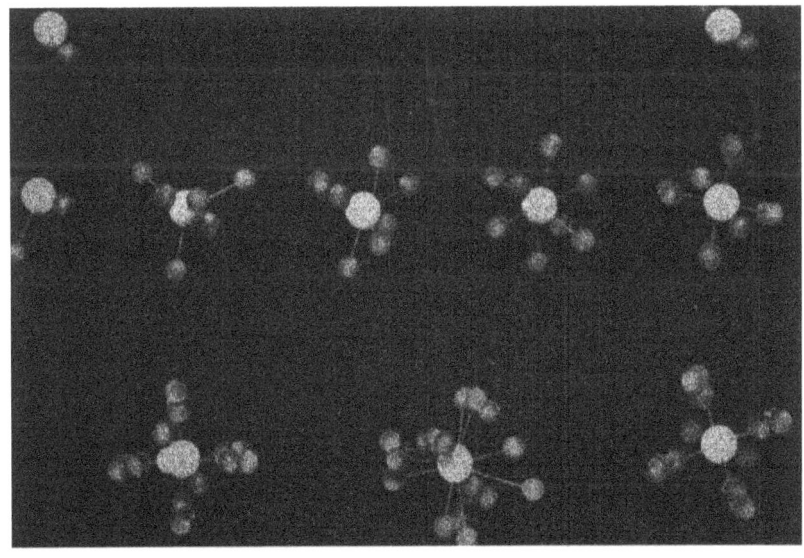

B. Models of atoms with electrons.

ATOMS OF WHICH THINGS ARE MADE

far to one side so that it acquires a greater speed than before, by the time it reaches the stationary set its momentum will carry it through. If the speed is very great, it shows no appreciable change in its motion due to its passing (Fig. 3, *c*); if the speed is rather less, it often suffers in going through (Fig. 3, *b*). It comes out less vigorous than when it went in; often it has changed the direction of motion also, and it has obviously left energy behind, for the magnets of the stationary set are left quivering. This happens no matter which pole of the swinging magnet is the lower, and clearly the same effect would be shown if the single swinging magnet were replaced by a more complicated set of nucleus and attendant satellites.

The behaviour of the model helps us to anticipate what we should find when atoms of our new design come across one another. If they approach at a moderate speed, they may rebound from one another; at a high speed they go through each other, and the higher the speed, the greater the chance of a passage without any obvious result. But there is always the chance that the nucleus of the moving atom may go so near to the nucleus of the atom through which it is passing that it experiences a perceptible deflection. The smaller the nuclei are, the less likely it is that this will happen.

You will have guessed already that you have actually seen such deflections as these in the kinematograph picture, such as also are shown in Plate III A to C. The tracks of the helium atom are quite straight in the main, but there are decided breaks in the straight lines, usually not more than one or two in each track. They are found mainly towards the finish. This is what might be expected, since the motion will then be slower. Several of them appear in Plate III A; a very good example of this kind of track is reproduced on a large scale in Plate III C. The upper track shows a slight but sharp deflection at a little distance from the end of its course, and a more pronounced deflection further on. Nearly every track shows some deviations at the very end. Thus the new conception of atomic structure explains all the effects in a satisfactory way.

It is strange to think of an atom as being empty as a solar system: not a round, hard and absolutely impenetrable body, but a combination of nucleus and electrons which occupies a certain space somewhat as an army occupies a country. The bodies of the soldiers do not fill the country from boundary to boundary; but enemy soldiers may not enter nevertheless.

ATOMS OF WHICH THINGS ARE MADE 35

These very characteristic pictures are the fruit of much watching and photographing. Breaks are found at every expansion, but it may be necessary to wait for a really good one. A very fine picture is shown in Plate III D. It is due to Mr. P. Blackett. In this case, helium was used instead of air. The nucleus of the flying helium atom, in traversing a helium atom belonging to the gas, has made an almost direct hit on the nucleus of the stationary atom : it has cannoned off it, as a billiard player would say. Both atoms now move with not unequal speeds, and both make fog tracks, as the figure shows. In Plate III c if we look carefully, we see that there is a minute spur on the last bend of the track already mentioned, which means that in this case an atom of oxygen or nitrogen has deflected the helium atom and has recoiled in consequence. Its track is very short, because it is much heavier than the atom which struck it, and, therefore, the velocity given to it has been comparatively small.

There is a certain curious feature to be found in some of the photographs which may well be explained. In some of the tracks there are gaps, as if the fog settling had failed. This is indeed the actual fact : there is no moisture to settle, because a helium atom has gone that way some very short time before and has used up the moisture in the neighbourhood. In Plate III B several tracks due to radium emanation are shown. They seem to start from anywhere in the chamber because the atoms of the emanation have wandered about the chamber before blowing up.

The next question that arises is as to the number of electron satellites which each atom possesses. Here we come to a very beautiful and remarkable feature of the new discoveries. It is not necessary to explain in full how it was discovered; we will be content with describing it.

In the atom as we now have it the nucleus is charged with positive electricity, the amount of the charge being just enough to neutralise the negative charges on the attendant electrons. All electrons, as we have already seen, are alike. We find that atoms differ in the number of attendants which they can maintain, and that the statement of that number describes the atom completely so far as its attitude towards other atoms is concerned. For instance, the atom of carbon can hold six electrons; the positive charge on the nucleus is the counterpart of six standard negative charges. Every atom which can retain six electrons is a carbon atom: no other definition of the carbon atom is required. Just so the "seven-electron" atom is nitrogen, the "eight-

ATOMS OF WHICH THINGS ARE MADE 37

electron" is oxygen and so on. All numbers are found in nature, with very few exceptions, from the "one-electron" atom—hydrogen—up to the "ninety-two-electron" atom—uranium. The missing numbers will probably be found some day; more or less accidentally, it may well be.

We may use models as a rough illustration of the point. The nucleus (Plate IV B) is represented by a white ball of solid rubber, the electrons by smaller balls forming the heads of pins which are stuck into the centre ball. The pins may be of different lengths (p. 77).

It is strange that the immense variety in Nature can be resolved into a series of numbers. It was at one time thought that the various sorts of atoms owed this variety to something more than that; it is a great surprise to find such a simple kind of difference between atom and atom. The unchanging feature of any particular sort of atom is the positive charge of electricity on the nucleus. It is in consequence of this that the proper number of electrons gather round. We may expect that they will arrange themselves in some fashion; we shall see later that they certainly do so. The sort of arrangement they take in each case, and the nature of the forces put into it, are very difficult questions, most of which we may well put to one side for the present, contenting ourselves with one or two simple aspects of the problem.

In the first place, it is interesting to watch the assembling of the little vertical magnets floating in the glass tank (Plate V A). They are buoyed up by ping-pong balls, painted black, and, so that we may see them easily, they carry white ping-pong balls at top. The magnets are all the same way up, so that naturally they repel one another and cluster round the edge of the basin. But there is an electromagnet underneath the bowl; which, when made active, draws the small magnets together. The arrangement in which they settle finally is governed partly by the pull towards the centre and partly by the mutual repulsions. Something of this kind must take place in the atom, but we must not push the analogy too closely, because the forces may be quite unlike those which are exerted in the model. We must content ourselves with observing that when there are only a few magnets afloat they group themselves in a ring; but when the number is increased they arrange themselves in concentric rings. A pretty effect is produced by putting in each additional magnet at the edge of the basin and watching it float away in a stately fashion to take its proper place.

PLATE V.

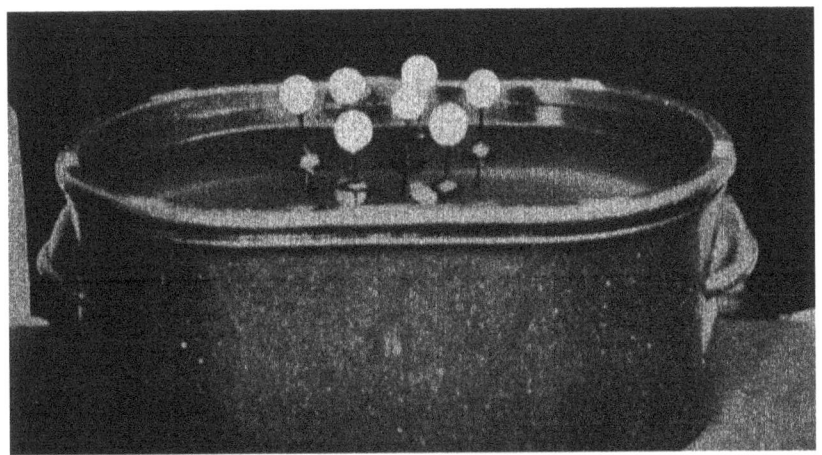

A. Floating magnets.

When the number of floating magnets is small, they form into a single ring, but when the number is increased, they form concentric rings.

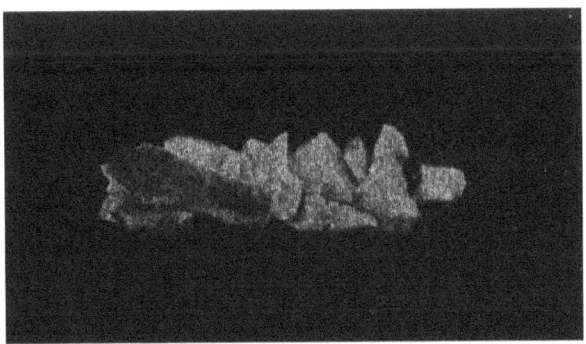

B. Crystals in tube containing emanation.

(From Prof. F. Soddy's "Interpretation of the Radium" (John Murray), by the kind permission of author and publisher.)

A similar division into concentric shells or groups is found in the arrangement of the electrons round the central nucleus of the atom. We will consider this more carefully in the next lecture. The experiment does not prove that there ought to be such an arrangement, but certainly suggests it.

We may now see more clearly what happens when the helium atom injures the atoms through which it passes and renders them attractive to the particles of moisture that form the fog. It is possible, in fact, for an atom to be deprived of one of its attendant electrons. Having lost one, it resists more strongly the loss of a second, still more of a third. As the helium atom goes on its way, it strips one atom after another of an attendant, and the electron set free goes off on a course of its own. But its separate life is very short-lived: it is soon attached to another atom. The atom that has lost an electron is now positively charged; the gainer is negatively charged. The two atoms would make things even again if they came sufficiently close together, and as they move about in the gas the negatives and the positives do in the end give and take electrons, and the whole gas is neutral once more.

There is a beautiful experiment with which we

may end this lecture. When the helium atoms strike certain substances they excite a phosphorescent glow. It is really, when we look into it closely, a set of minute flashes due to the impacts of the separate atoms; under a microscope the effect is as when we drop pebbles into a phosphorescent sea. The glass vessel (Plate V B) contains crystals that phosphoresce under the stimulus of the swift-moving helium atoms; one is kunzite, another zinc sulphide, another willemite. In another tube is a quantity of radium emanation: the gas which, you will remember, is the immediate descendant of radium itself. When it is released and is allowed to pass into the tubes containing the crystals the latter glow in brilliant colours. In the figure the crystals have been made to photograph themselves by their own phosphorescence.

The radium action has, we see, given us a remarkable insight into the structure of the atom, for which there is a general reason to be given. The student of science has long been familiar with the existence of various atoms and with their properties; he has never seen one, nor the effects of one. He has handled atoms in crowds only. When the chemist causes elements to form compounds, or analyses compounds into elements, he

ATOMS OF WHICH THINGS ARE MADE

deals with enormous numbers of atoms in any operation big enough to see. But in this radioactive effect we observe the action of one atom at a time, and here lies the secret of the advance. The speed of the helium projectile, a hundred thousand times the speed with which the atoms move ordinarily when they form part of a gas, gives the individual atom the power of making itself felt. When we look at the fog tracks, we see the actions of separate atoms; we see something which would have filled the early defenders of the atomic theory with astonishment and pleasure. One atom of helium passes through one atom of oxygen, let us say; and comes out on the other side, and both may bear evidences of the encounter. Effectively we use such evidence to help us to determine the nature of the atoms. The helium atom is like a spy that has gone into a foreign country and has come out again with a tale to tell.

LECTURE II

THE NATURE OF GASES

WE have seen that all things are made of about ninety kinds of atoms, and that in them is wrapped up the mystery and the infinite variety of the material world. In each there is a nucleus which is positively charged; round the nucleus are electrons which are units of negative electricity. The positive charge of the nucleus is a multiple of a certain unit charge, equal to the charge on the electron, but of opposite sign. The number of electrons which every atom possesses under normal conditions is an exact balance to the positive charge on the nucleus, so that the atom as a whole is not charged; its positive and negative charges balance. Whether or no the electrons are revolving round the central nucleus like planets round a sun, or whether they possess other more complicated motions are not matters of importance to us for the moment. Something is known of these points, but the whole question is difficult. The only consequences of this strange arrange-

THE NATURE OF GASES

ment of nucleus and electrons which we must consider can be drawn without thinking about the possible motions. One consequence is that the atoms do not encroach on each others' domains under ordinary circumstances. Each has an outer cloak or shell of electrons; and when two atoms are brought close together there is a resisting force which we may suppose to be due to the mutual repulsion of the two shells. But when two atoms are hurled at each other with sufficient speed the outer defences may be broken down and the atoms pass through each other. When this happens the atoms may afterwards disentangle themselves and pass on their way as if there had been no encounter at all : one or both may have suffered the loss of an electron or two, but the damage is soon made good. It is only when the nucleus of one approaches sufficiently close to the nucleus of the other that there is a change of motion like that due to the meeting of two balls. Changes of this kind are so rare and imply such a closeness of approach that we are bound to think of the nucleus as very small indeed. These penetrations of atomic domains are brought to our notice by the actions of radium and similar substances, as explained in the first lecture, and are of importance to us because they make us realise the empty nature of the atom, and its sun and planet structure. They do not occur in the usual relations of atoms to one another, because the speed is far too small. The domain which the atom occupies to the exclusion of others is about a hundred millionth of an inch across; it is within this minute space that the nucleus and the electrons perform their relative motions. The light atoms have smaller domains, and the heavier somewhat larger: a factor of three or four will take us from the smallest to the largest.

I have said that all atoms are in motion, and that there is a constant struggle between some form of attractive force which would draw all the atoms together and this motion which would keep them independent. The existence of an attractive force which we here take into account as something very important does not at first seem to be reconcilable with the atomic structure we have just considered, because in this we supposed that the outer shells of electrons would prevent the atoms from coming too close to each other. It is a difficult point, because both views are certainly correct. It is, no doubt, our present ignorance of the nature of these forces that prevents us from arriving at a clear understanding. We have seen how it can happen that when two atoms approach each other at great speeds they go through one another, while at moderate speeds they bound off each other like two billiard balls. We have to go a step further, and see how, at very slow speeds of approach, they may actually stick together. We have all seen those swinging gates which, when their swing is considerable, go to and fro without locking When the swing has declined, however, the latch suddenly drops into its place, the gate is held and after a short rattle the motion is all over. We have to explain an effect something like that. When the two atoms meet, the repulsions of their electron shells usually cause them to recoil; but if the motion is small and the atoms spend a longer time in each other's neighbourhood, there is time for something to happen in the internal arrangements of both atoms, like the drop of the gate-latch into its socket, and the atoms are held. It all depends on some structure of the atom which causes a want of uniformity over its surface, so that there is usually a repulsion; but the repulsion will be turned into attraction if the two atoms are allowed time to make the necessary arrangements, or even if at the outset they are presented to each other in the right way. We shall see later several very interesting examples of this effect.

We are going to consider in this lecture the case when the attractive forces between the atoms do not act, whether from want of time, or from feebleness, or from any other reason. A crowd of atoms is, when this is the case, a gas.

Such cases are very numerous. In particular there are certain atoms which furnish notable examples; they are nos. 2, 10, 18, 36, 54, 86: that is to say, they are those in which the nuclei possess positive charges whose magnitudes are represented by one or other of these numbers, and which normally possess negative electrons to match. These atoms have only the feeblest desire to join up with each other. They do not enter into combination with atoms of other kinds; in other words, they do not form chemical compounds. We may call them the "unsociable" atoms. They take no obvious part in the doings of the world, and their existence was entirely overlooked until a few years ago. It was only when the late Lord Rayleigh was making careful measurements of the weight of nitrogen obtained from various sources that he noted a small but unmistakable discrepancy between the density of nitrogen as prepared from the break-up of a known compound of nitrogen and the density of what was left of air when every known gas had

THE NATURE OF GASES

been abstracted from it. According to the view held at the time of his experiment, the residue should have been pure nitrogen. As a matter of fact, atmospheric air contains a small percentage of one of these "unsociable" atoms or gases; it is no. 18, that which has eighteen units of positive electricity in the nucleus. So Rayleigh's very careful measurements led to the discovery of the hitherto unknown substance. It was named argon, the "lazy one." Perhaps the name does not express its chief characteristic; for the atom is as quick in its movements as any other of its own size. The weight of the air in the lecture-room of the Royal Institution is about 15 cwt.; it contains about 18 lb. of argon. If the gas had had the least tendency to form any chemical association, such an amount, though relatively small, would have been easily detected by the delicate analytical methods of chemistry.

The atom of helium, the smallest of the series, is identical with the atom expelled by radium and other radioactive substances in the act of disintegration. It has two electrons normally; though as it flies through matter when radium has ejected it its complement of electrons is apt to be torn away for the time. The positive charge on the nucleus is not affected by the flight, so that when the atom comes to the end of it, the deficiency in electrons is quickly repaired : there are always stray electrons to be picked up. Then the atom takes up the quiet and independent existence which is its characteristic. Perhaps most of the helium in the world has at some time been fired off, atom by atom, from radioactive substances. At any rate, it is found in places where such actions must have occurred. Helium is now collected in large quantities in America and Canada, where it is found bubbling up in certain springs. It is used for filling dirigible balloons, for which purpose its main properties make it most suitable. It is light, and its lifting power is almost as great as that of hydrogen, the one-electron atom; the atomic weight increases on the whole with the number of electrons. The lifting power of a gas, we must remember, depends not on the density of the gas, but on the difference between the density of the gas and the density of the air. The densities of hydrogen, helium, and air are in the proportion 1 : 2 : 14·4; the lifting powers of hydrogen and helium are in the proportion 13·4 to 12·4. But its main virtue is that it is not inflammable. The hydrogen atom is very sociable, and in particular has a violent desire to become associated with oxygen : if hydrogen and

THE NATURE OF GASES

oxygen are mixed, it needs but a spark to start the combination, with fire and explosion as the result. A hydrogen-filled balloon is therefore liable to disaster; but helium seeks no change, and there is no danger from fire. The name of the gas is due to its discovery in the sun; a bright line in the sun's spectrum could not be identified with lines due to any of the known elements on the earth. The name " helium," or " sun-substance," was therefore given to the unknown substance to which the line was due. It was at a later date that helium was found to be a member of the series of gases which Lord Rayleigh and Sir William Ramsay were led to examine as the consequence of Rayleigh's nitrogen experiments.

The ten-electron atom neon, the " new one," is less common than argon. It has a peculiar property of glowing easily and brightly under the stimulus of electric discharge, and is often used in electric light bulbs : we have all observed the reddish-orange glow of the neon lamp.

Krypton (36), the " hidden one," and " xenon " (54), the " stranger," are very rare. The last of the series, with eighty-six electrons normally, is the heavier fragment of the break-up of the radium atom. Like the rest, it tends to pursue an independent existence, so that radium, when it breaks up, turns into two gases. In some of the Wilson pictures (Plate III A, B) of the tracks of the helium atoms we may see a track that begins in the middle of the chamber: it is due to the break-up, in its turn, of an atom of this heavy gas, for it also is radioactive. In fact, its average length of life is only three and a half days.

We must not suppose that these strange atoms cannot be made to associate together under any circumstances. It is possible to make them join together as a liquid, but only at extremely low temperatures. At ordinary temperatures they are all gases. The liquefaction of helium is one of the achievements of the laboratory of Kamerlingh Onnes at Leiden, where the production of low temperatures has been carried to a very great state of efficiency.

There are certain other atoms—hydrogen, nitrogen, oxygen and others—which readily form into small companies, or molecules, each of which is almost as free from any desire to associate itself with other molecules of the same kind and, in many cases, of other kinds as the atoms of helium and argon. Two atoms of hydrogen make a very stable and "unsociable" molecule; so do two atoms of nitrogen, or of oxygen. In these cases, the properties of the substance are at ordinary temperatures those of a gas. The liquefaction of hydrogen was accomplished by Sir James Dewar in the laboratories of this Institution; the machinery is still here. In the ante-room there is a picture which shows Dewar pouring liquid hydrogen from one of his vacuum flasks into another during the course of a lecture which he is giving in this room. The air consists mainly of a mixture of oxygen and nitrogen molecules. Other well-known molecules which form gases under ordinary circumstances are carbon monoxide (CO), carbon dioxide (CO_2), methane (CH_4), and so on. In all these cases when two of these molecules meet one another at speeds which are proper to ordinary temperatures they recoil from the impact, and so maintain an independent existence. What we have now to consider are the consequences we should expect to follow from this condition of independence.

Let us imagine a closed vessel containing a number of atoms or molecules moving about within it—containing a gas, as we should say. They continually meet one another and the walls of the vessel, and behave as a number of billiard balls set in motion on a table would do if their motion were frictionless and therefore perpetual. In fact, it is convenient to use a small billiard table as an illustration, and Messrs. Burroughs and Watts have very kindly given us one for the purpose. The balls soon come to rest on the table, because the cushions, as well as the balls, are not perfectly elastic; moreover, there are losses by friction as the balls run over the cloth, smooth though it is. Nevertheless, the motion, once started, lasts long enough to give an idea of what must happen if it were maintained indefinitely.

It is natural to ask how the force of gravity would affect the movement of the atoms in our closed vessel. Would it not bring them all to the bottom? Why should the gas fill the upper as well as the lower parts of the vessel? The answer is that gravity certainly has its effect in full, but it is so very small as to be unobservable in our particular case. If we might imagine that all the heat were taken from the gas, and its movements therefore ceased, and if the attractive

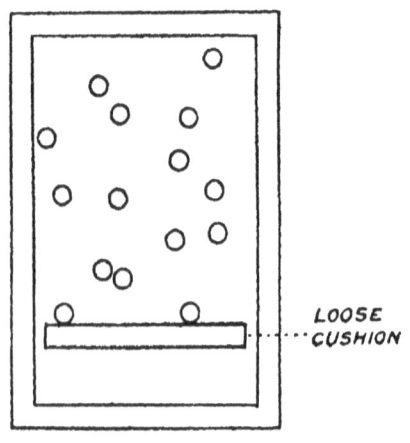

FIG. 4.—Diagram of small experimental billiard table, with balls and loose cushion.

If the balls are in motion they drive the loose cushion before them and they lose some of their energy. If, on the other hand, the cushion is suddenly advanced, the energy of the motion of the balls is increased.

THE NATURE OF GASES

forces could be ignored, the atoms would, of course, lie about at rest on the bottom of the vessel. If a very little heat were now given to them, we might imagine them to begin dancing up and down, like perfectly elastic balls on a perfectly elastic floor. If the rise were a thousandth of a degree Fahrenheit, they would bounce to a height of about seven inches. With enough heat they would begin to hit the top of the vessel as well; we might suppose them to be so few that they did not hit each other very often. But at ordinary temperatures their movements would be so rapid—something like 6000 ft. a second—that gravity would make little difference in their velocity as they ascended and descended, and there would be, at any moment, as many at the top as at the bottom of the vessel. If they were as numerous as the molecules of the air under ordinary conditions, they would hit each other more often than the walls. In the air, the usual length of path between two successive encounters with other molecules is only about four-millionths of an inch. Since gravity has no obvious effect, the billiard table is all the better an illustration; we might find an analogy to gravity by giving it a slight tilt, but it would not be worth while doing so.

If the atoms or molecules of a gas are continually hitting the walls, the latter must always experience an outward pressure: we speak, in fact, of the pressure of a gas upon its envelope. The distension of a balloon is due to the bombardment of the covering by the molecules. If we put a loose cushion on our table and make the balls roll about, the cushion is driven backwards. If there were twice as many balls as there are, there would be twice as much pressure. This is the well-known gas law that pressure is proportional to density, other things being kept the same. We increase the pressure on the cushions if we make the balls move faster; in the same way, the pressure of a gas rises with the temperature.

Suppose now that I suddenly advance this loose cushion while the balls are moving and striking it. It is obvious that the motion of the balls is increased. In the same way, if one of the walls of the gas vessel is pushed in, as when a piston is forced deeper into a cylinder, the motion of the atoms is increased. In other words, the temperature is raised. We all know how hot a bicycle pump becomes when we use it to force air into a tyre. The converse is equally true. If the cushion on our table is

THE NATURE OF GASES

withdrawn as the balls strike it, their motion is diminished. If we have played cricket, we know that when we want to catch a ball we must draw our hands back as the ball begins to touch them : the retreating hands destroy the motion of the ball gradually. If we hold them in a fixed position, the ball is sure to jump out again. So also when a lacrosse player catches a ball, he draws his crosse downwards when the ball first enters it, and makes the stopping of the ball an operation lasting over two or three feet of its path. A tennis racquet can be used to catch a tennis ball in the same way, but the action must be well timed, because the racquet face is so stiff. In the case of the gas, the corresponding effect is its chilling by expansion. We had an example in the use of Mr. Wilson's apparatus, where the sudden enlargement of a space full of moist air caused such a chill that the moisture settled as a fog on the tracks of the helium atoms. The expansion had to be fairly sudden, because if it had been otherwise there would have been time for heat to flow in from outside during the action, and the desired low temperature would not have been reached.

The expansion of great masses of air in the atmosphere is a frequent source of rain and snow.

In the constant movement of the winds it may happen that some huge volume of damp air expands into a space where the pressure has been lowered and becomes so cold that the water vapour begins to condense. It is easy to repeat the experiment on a small scale. The glass tube which we see on the table (Plate VI B) contains air which has become charged with moisture which it bubbled through water on its way to fill the tube. The road by which it came is now closed by a tap. At the other end of the tube is a second tap, which at the moment is closed and cuts off the tube from a connection with a vacuum pump. If this second tap is opened, the air in the tube expands, and at once a white mist fills the tube. A beam from the lantern passes down the tube and lights up the mist. We may allow the air to be drawn off by the vacuum pump: and we can repeat the experiment as often as we like. Every time that we fill the tube with damp air which has been filtered from all suspended particles of dirt and smoke, we get the same sort of white mist that we see sometimes in the clean country. But if we allow the air from the room to flow directly into the tube without being filtered, the expansion produces a dense fog, such as London air is

PLATE VI.

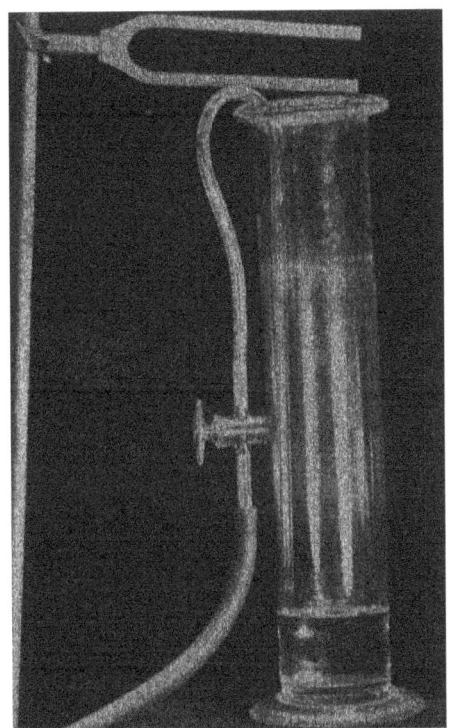

A. Tuning fork over jar.

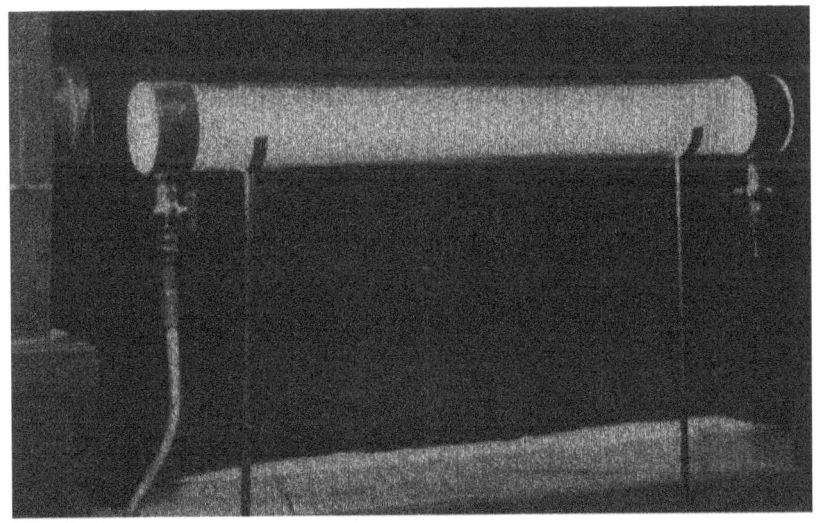

B. Fog apparatus.
The long glass tube is full of fog.

THE NATURE OF GASES

ready to produce at any time, as we know only too well.

There are other properties of a gas which the billiard table will help us to understand. Let us mix with the ordinary billiard balls a number of light ping-pong balls, and set the whole lot in motion. We see at once that in the general movement the ping-pong balls acquire greater velocities than the others. Just so if a gas contains two kinds of atom, one heavy and one light, the latter, in the constant interchange of motions, acquires a higher average speed than the former. When hydrogen is mixed with oxygen, the hydrogen molecules actually move four times as fast as the oxygen molecules on the average. A calculation, into which we do not enter, tells us that atoms which mix with one another all possess the same average energy, the lighter making up for their deficiency in weight by an excess of velocity. Even if the gases are not mixed, but are contained in separate vessels, the same rule holds, provided that the gases are at the same temperature. Although the atoms of the two gases cannot interchange and balance their energies directly, they do so in effect by way of the various kinds of matter which reach from one to the other, by the walls of the vessels, by the table on which perhaps they both stand, and by the atmosphere. In fact, the average motion of the atom is fixed by the temperature.

We can easily find an illustration of this effect. Sound is a movement which is handed on from atom to atom in a gas through which the sound is passing, just as a chain of workers pass buckets of water to a fire. The quicker the workers move their hands and arms, the quicker the water moves. Just so sound travels faster the greater the velocities of the atoms; or, what comes to the same thing, the lighter the atoms. An organ pipe blown with coal gas gives a higher note than when it is blown with air, because the molecules of the lighter gas move more quickly and the vibrations of the pipe are more frequent. A simple experiment will help to make this clear. On the table is a glass jar, into which water has been poured until the air column which is left responds loudly to the motion of a tuning-fork held over it (Plate VI A). The air waves pass up and down the jar in exact time with the oscillations of the fork; the natural period of the jar is the same as the note of the fork, as I can tell by blowing gently across the top of the jar and so drawing a whispering note from it. I now introduce gas into the jar through an india-rubber

THE NATURE OF GASES

tube, and the response fades away. Movements now pass up and down the jar more quickly, and the natural period of the jar is no longer that of the fork. If I now pour out some of the water in the jar and begin again with a filling of air, there is no response to the fork until I put in a certain amount of gas. Then the note swells out as soon as the mixture is such that the timing of the gas movement in the jar agrees with the periodicity of the tuning-fork.

Let us imagine, again, that a very small hole is made in the walls of a vessel which contains a gas. Every time that an atom, or molecule, as the case may be, strikes the hole it passes out and never comes back. It is clear that a light gas will leak away more quickly than a heavy gas, because its atoms are moving about in the vessel at a greater rate, and a larger number will strike the hole every second. This effect is frequently employed to separate two gases, when other means are ineffective. For example, Rayleigh and Ramsay used it to separate argon from nitrogen, the mixture of the two being the residue of the atmospheric air when all other gases had been removed. The mixture was made to flow along a series of clay tobacco-pipe stems, and the nitrogen leaked out through the pores of the pipes more quickly than the argon. The argon atom is forty times as heavy as the hydrogen atom, and the nitrogen molecule twenty-eight times; the nitrogen therefore leaks away more quickly through the porous clay walls of the pipe stem, and the gas that issues from the other end of the pipe system is richer in argon than the mixture which entered it. The process of diffusion of one gas into another is really the same in character, because the gaps between the atoms or molecules of one gas are to be compared with the pores in the clay pipe. Diffusion is a very slow action, in spite of the fact that the atoms are moving so quickly, the reason being that encounters are so numerous. One is apt to think that one gas diffuses into another quickly: on such evidence as that, if a gas tap is left open, the smell of the gas is quickly perceived all over the room. This dispersion is, however, due to convection currents rather than to diffusion, streams of the house gas running in concentrated form through the air. The effect is beautifully seen in the mounting of smoke from a cigarette (Plate VII). If the cigarette is laid down on the ash-tray a fine stream of blue smoke rises in a waving pencil, which becomes spread and bent and twisted into delicate spirals and curved surfaces. As the

PLATE VII.

A

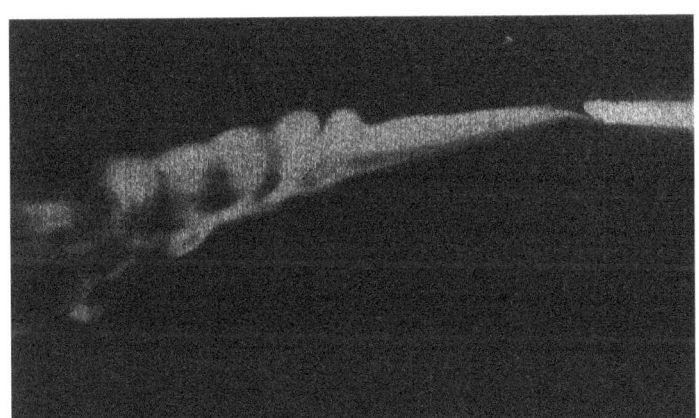

B

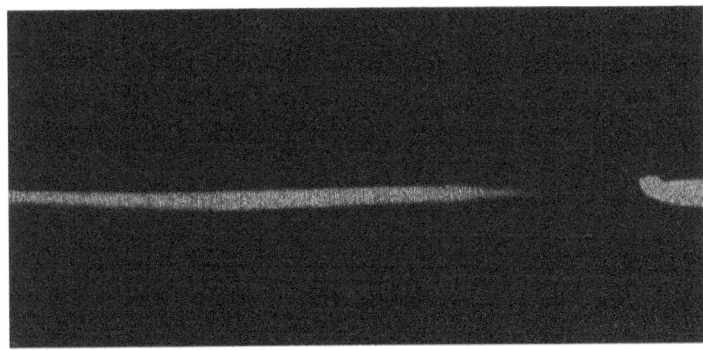

C

Cigarette smoke.

A. The smoke of the cigarette is rising in a straight column. The air all round is being dragged up with it, though the photograph cannot show it; there is a rising stream of which the smoke marks the centre. B. and C. Here the cigarette has been suddenly moved just before the photograph was taken. The streams of rising air that first met at the cigarette point and went up side by side are rolling and twisting over one another, preserving their identity. They do not mix, except very slowly by means of the diffusion of particles from one stream to another, though the particles are in motion, otherwise the smoke would be a shapeless mass. Meeting streams of air become mixed by convection rather than diffusion.

THE NATURE OF GASES 61

stream mingles finally with the air, it gives an example of convection. Diffusion between the smoke-laden air stream and the pure air is taking place also all the time; but the process is so slow that the edges of the clouds remain sharply defined for a long time. So also when a room is warmed by hot air, the distribution of the heat is due to convection currents, streams of hot air percolating through the cold. It is not due to the molecules of the hot air making their way individually through the molecules of the cold; that goes on, but its progress is slow. Convection is more effective than conduction.

Movements of bodies of hot gas in a cold are, of course, governed by the laws of gravity: the lighter body, if it keeps together, tends to rise in the heavier. The smoke of the cigarette rises because the air over the glowing end is warmed and made light; colder currents run in from all round and, meeting each other, rise together round the thin sheet of smoke. The thin sheet is their joint boundary; if the air is still and the currents are steady the upright column grows long; but a slight movement of the cigarette upsets the even flow, and the column breaks into beautiful curves. The action of a chimney in the formation of a draught is, no doubt, known to every one; but it may be interesting to look again at an old experiment of Faraday's. A little spirit on some tow is lighted and held over the mouth of the shorter limb of the bent tube in the figure. By blowing for a moment the flame is made to go down the short limb and up the long one; once started on the downward direction it does not change when the blowing stops. The flues of grates in hospital wards are often built on this plan, the draught going under the floor. The movement is, of course, due to the fact that the hot air in the long limb is lighter than a corresponding volume of the air outside. The reverse happens sometimes in the house when the chimney is colder than the air outside, and a down draught brings a sooty smell into the room.

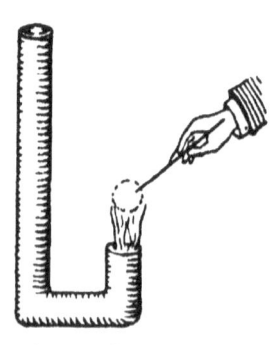

FIG. 5.—Reproduced from Faraday's *Chemistry of a Candle.*

Something nearer to a conduction process takes place when the gas in a vessel is heated through the walls. The molecules when they come to the wall in the course of their movement receive impulses from the vibrations of the solid material, somewhat in the same way as the ball in the

THE NATURE OF GASES 63

figure receives a violent knock from the vibrating prong of the tuning fork.

When Sir James Dewar designed the " vacuum

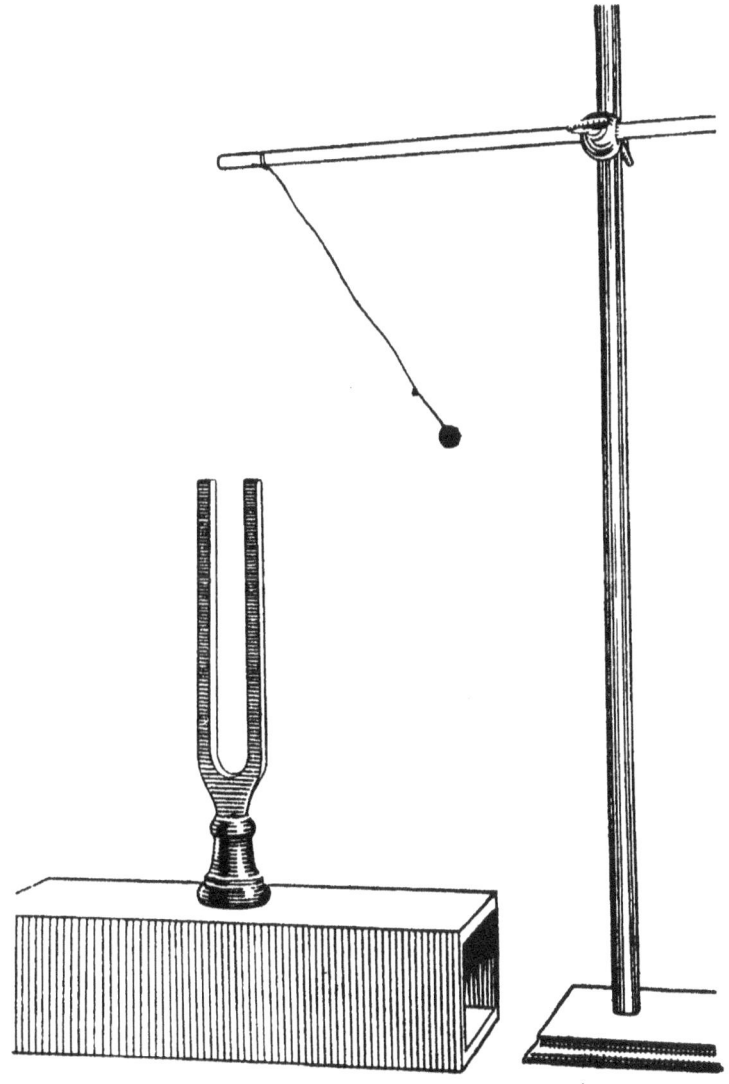

FIG. 6.—Tuning fork and pith ball.
The pith ball is hurled violently from the vibrating fork.

flask" to hold his liquid air, he made a double-walled glass vessel and extracted the air from between the walls. He left no molecules to pick up energy from the outer wall and carry it to the inner. No heat could be conveyed to the liquid air by conduction or by convection. Heat can also travel by radiation through the ether;

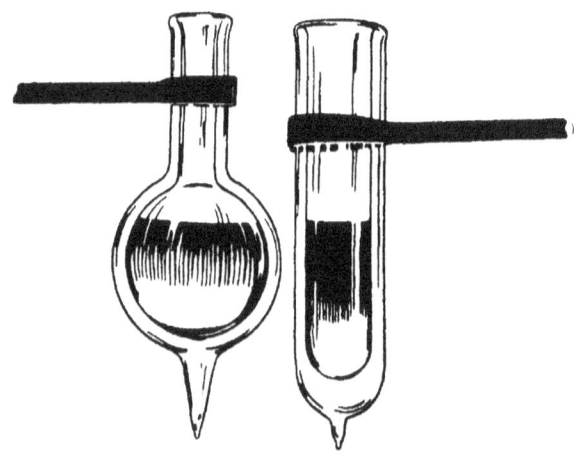

FIG. 7.—Vacuum flask.

Observe the tube at the bottom (now sealed off) through which the air has been drawn from between the inner and outer glass of each flask.

but this can be stopped by silvering the glass surfaces inside the double walls. When this is done the isolation of the air is almost perfect.

The entire independence of the atoms or molecules of a gas gives it perfect divisibility. When we cut a solid body with a knife we have to exert a force to tear the molecules from one another; but such binding forces in a gas are

PLATE VIII

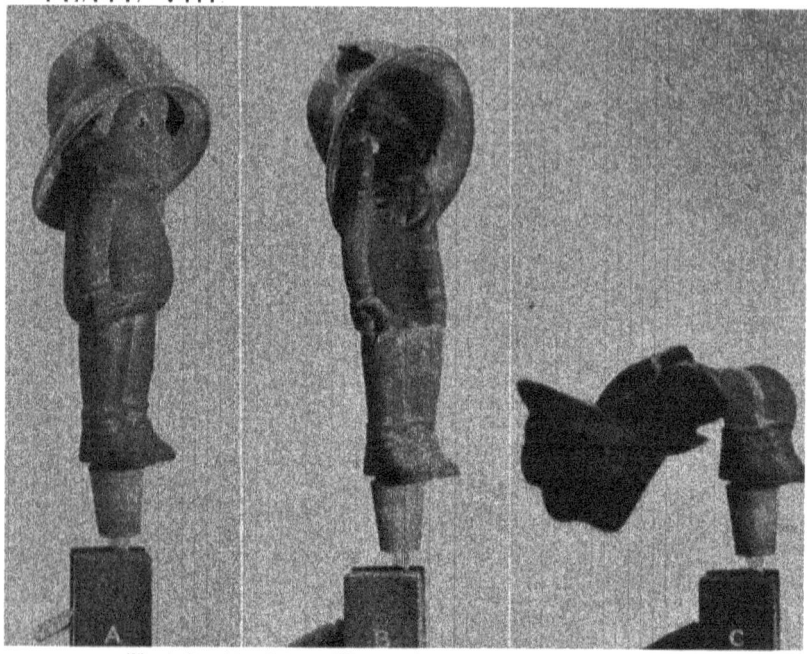

The indiarubber figure collapses when connected to the vacuum pump.

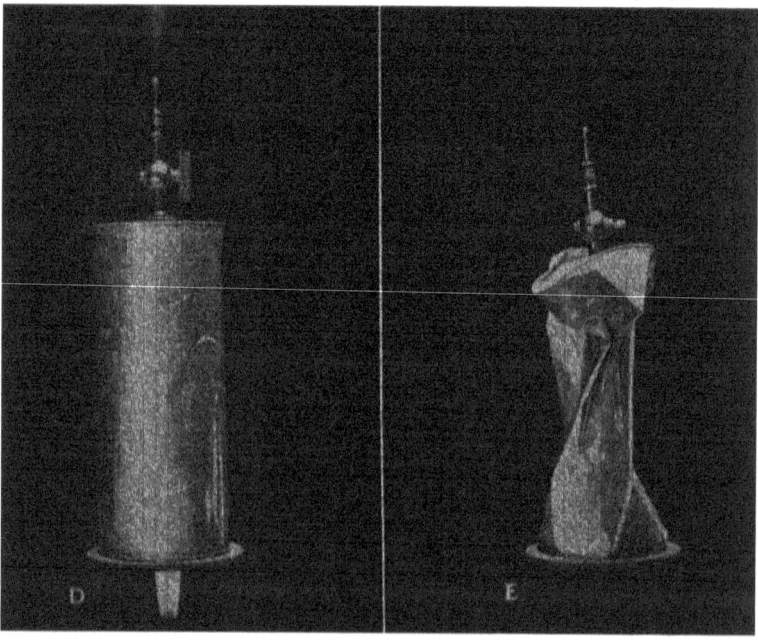

The water in the tin was boiling vigorously when the Bunsen burner was removed and the stop-cock closed. When cold water was poured over it, it collapsed.

THE NATURE OF GASES

negligible. If anything is moving through the air it experiences a resistance only because it is necessary to set some of the air in motion, and this requires the expenditure of energy. Gases are light, of course, and the energy required to move them is correspondingly small. The lightness of the air and the ease with which we pass through it make it easy to forget both how great is the pressure of the air at the surface of the earth and how weighty is the air in any large space such as this room. The air exerts a pressure of about a ton on every square foot of our bodies; that we do not collapse under it is due to the fact that any air within our bodies is at practically the same pressure as the air outside. The little rubber figure in the illustration (Plate VIII A) collapses utterly if its air content is withdrawn. The thin tin vessel shown in Plate VIII B has at first contained some water which has been raised to the boil so that the steam has driven out all the air. The opening by which the steam is issuing is closed, and some cold water is then poured over the vessel. The steam within condenses, and the pressure falls to almost nothing. The tin vessel then crumples up under the pressure from outside. Perhaps the magnitude of air pressure is brought home to us in an even more striking way when we consider that an iron bar, **one** square inch in section and nearly five feet long, when resting erect on the table, exerts of its own weight no more pressure on the square inch of the table with which it is in contact than the air does.

If we take into sufficient account, therefore, the weight of the air, it is not surprising that it takes a great force to set it in swift motion, or that, when moving rapidly, it can exert great pressure on any body which stands in its road. We all are familiar with the pressure of the wind, and know what havoc a gale may cause. So also the revolving aeroplane screw drives back a mass of air at a high speed, and the large force of reaction gives the necessary speed to the plane. Again, when it is on the wing, the plane, like a bird, is continually tending to fall and to carry with it masses of air beneath and around it. But it takes force to set such air masses in motion, and the reaction gives the uplift to the plane. If the plane had no forward motion it would quickly create a downward movement in the air below it, and fall with it; but it is always riding on to new masses of air which have not begun to fall. A simple little experiment illustrates the point. A piece of paper of any convenient size,

THE NATURE OF GASES

say three inches by one, is launched as the figure shows; it turns over and over and reaches the ground along a sloping path. The direction of the turning is related to that of the sliding, in the same way as that of a ball running down the *under* side of an inclined plane. The explanation is that the leading edge of the paper runs on to new air which has not begun to fall, whereas the following half of the paper is on air which has

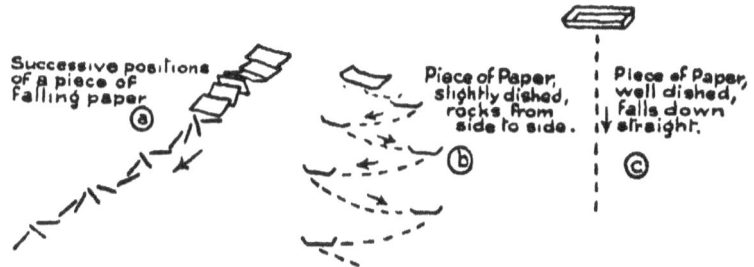

FIG. 8.—Pieces of paper of various forms fluttering to the ground.

started to move downwards because the leading edge was lately resting on it. So the following half falls and the leading half does not, which makes the paper turn, as the illustration shows, until the paper begins to move forward again. But now the edge which was following becomes the leading edge, and vice versa.

The paper turns over and over, its very simple shape being the cause of the motion. Now, a bird or an aeroplane when gliding moves in a steady, stately fashion, and the design of the wing is in reality anything but simple, as builders of aeroplanes have found. The exact form of the plane—it is not indeed a plane at all—and especially of the leading edge, is full of subtle importance. A bird's wings are used not only for gliding, but also for flapping, and there is a

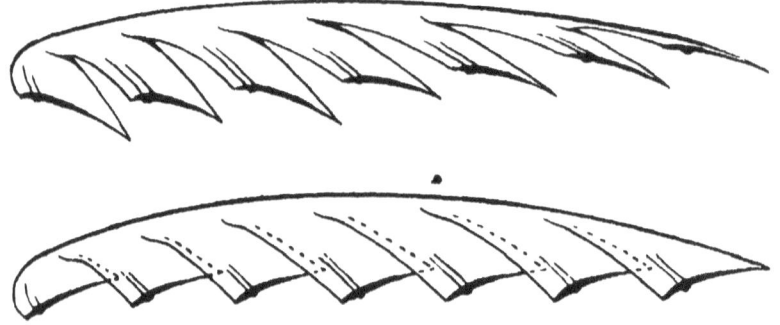

FIG. 9.—Drawings, after Lilienthal, showing feathers opening to let the air through on the up-stroke (upper drawing), and closed to hold the air on the down-stroke (lower drawing).

beautiful mechanism which adapts them for their special purpose. The wing is, in fact, a set of valves, which open when the wing rises and close when it descends; so that there is less pressure on the wing in the up-stroke than in the down. The action is something like that of the webbed foot of a duck, which opens out and exerts a greater pressure on the water as the foot is kicked back than when it is being drawn forward; but the mode of action is quite different. The rib of the feather does not always lie in the centre, but is often well to one side, and a row of feathers is so arranged that they overlap and turn somewhat on their ribs. When the wing is lifted they open like a louvred window and the air passes through; when the wing is forced down they close, pressing tight against each other. The two drawings of Fig. 9 A are adapted from

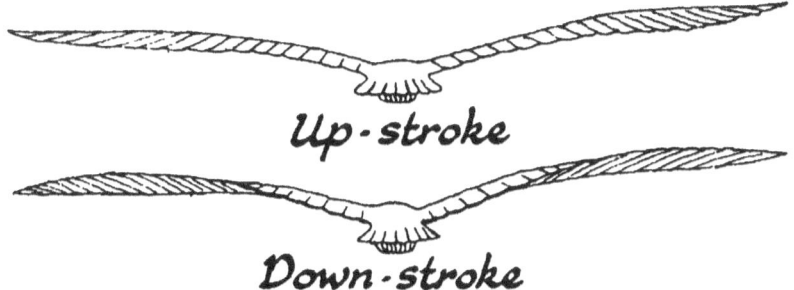

FIG. 9A.—Gull in flight. On the down-stroke the gull's wing has turned over showing the under side, thus giving a shove forward.

Otto Lilienthal's "Birdflight," p. 101. They are sections of the condor's wing. As Lilienthal says, "Every observer of the flight of storks knows that one is able to periodically see through the wings." Even the countless parts of each feather partake in this valve action. It is clear that with such a mechanism the mere flapping of the wings must give an uplift apart from all other characteristics of the motion. The forward thrust is due to the bending of the wing about its stiff leading edge, as may be seen from the two drawings of the wings of a gull in flight ("Birdflight," p. 96). They were made in the sunshine: as the wing rises, the hinder parts are turned down and show the bright upper surface; as the wing descends, it twists so as to show the darker under surface. It must also be true that even if the wings are held outstretched without motion there will be an uplift if the air is full of little motions, swirls and quiverings. The wonderful gliding of birds that travel for miles without a movement of the wings or any apparent effort may conceivably be connected with this effect; it is said that it does not take place when the air is perfectly still.

A very pretty example of the laws of the dynamics of the air is to be found in the swerve of a spinning ball; it is likely to interest most of those here. We see it and make use of it in nearly every game, though perhaps the golf ball shows it most, because its speed is greatest. Suppose that the golfer " slices " his ball: instead of pursuing a straight course in the direction in which it appeared to be struck, it curls away to the right. The ball is then spinning; the front of the ball is going from left to right of the golfer as he gazes after it, the back of the ball is going the other way. It is clear that he

THE NATURE OF GASES

has not hit the ball truly, but has drawn the head of the club across the ball; perhaps he pulled in his arms at the moment of striking and did not follow through properly. As the ball moves forward there is a dense cushion of air in front of it which has not had time to get away. If the ball is spinning as supposed, the left-hand side (the golfer being the observer) is spinning forwards in the direction of flight, the right-hand side is moving the opposite way, so far as spin goes. The consequence is that through friction the air on the left-hand side is carried forward more than on the right, and the cushion of air in front of the ball is denser on the left than on the right. Consequently the ball swerves to the right.

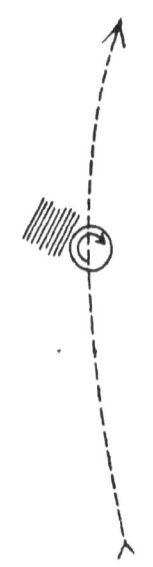

FIG. 10.—Flight of golf ball with "slice."

The shading shows where air is piled up by the ball as it spins and moves forward, and this accumulation makes the ball shear off to the right.

The long carry of a golf ball is always due to spin of the proper kind: the stroke must be so made that the ball is turning about a horizontal axis, the lowest part of the ball moving, so far as it is due to the spin, in the forward direction.

This makes the ball tend to rise as it flies. Sometimes we see it actually take a curved path which is convex to the ground. If it were not for this action the ball would not go half the distance that it does. If there were no air at all, we may observe, in addition, the carry of the ball would be two or three times greater than the normal, because its resistance to a high-speed ball is so great. We should drive a ball much further if

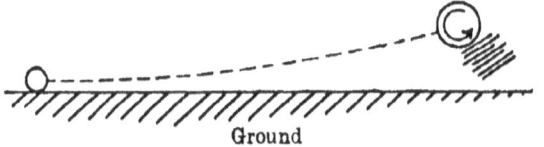

FIG. 11.—Regular flight of golf ball: a pocket of condensed air, shown by the shading in the drawing, keeps the ball up.

we could avoid the resistance from the air; but as we cannot do that, we take advantage of what may be done by giving the ball a spin.

The flight of a Rugby football, like that of the fast-spinning golf ball, is often curved upwards, when the kick has gone rather under the ball, and though, of course, it is most obvious when the kick is against the wind, yet I think it can be seen in still air. In tennis the player often draws his racquet over the top of the ball, giving it the opposite kind of spin, the top moving forwards faster than the bottom. This makes the ball

THE NATURE OF GASES

duck, so that, though hit very hard, it keeps in the court after passing the net. Heavy balls swerve less than light balls going at the same speed; yet we all know the swerve that can be given to a cricket ball, and the swerve that the pitcher can give in baseball is a marvellous spectacle. Of all ways of studying the effect, the simplest, perhaps, is by the use of toy balloons which nowadays are toughly made and will stand much knocking about. It is easy, by striking with the hand, or a racquet if preferred, to give any sort of spin that is desired and to observe all sorts of swerves and soarings and " dooks."

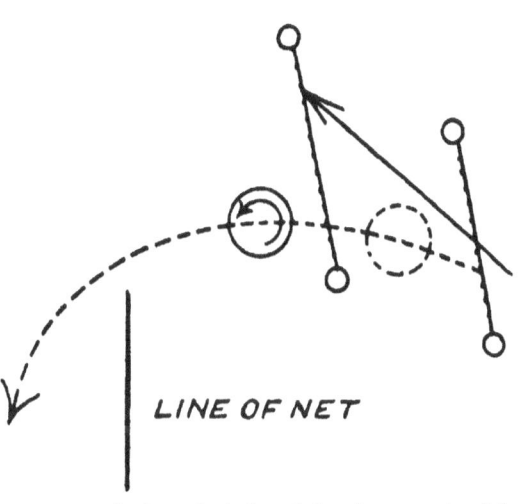

FIG. 12.—Action of stroke of tennis racquet, giving spin to the ball and making it drop quickly over the net (exaggerated).

On the right, section of racquet and ball before the stroke: arrow showing direction of motion of racquet.

The various examples of the properties of gases which we have been considering are all to be explained, as we have seen, on the hypothesis that some kinds of atoms have very little tendency to associate with other atoms, whether of the same or of other kinds : I have spoken of them as the " unsociable atoms." Other atoms, again, such as hydrogen or oxygen, though very sociable individually, tend to form more or less unsociable molecules. Thus the air consists of a mixture of unsociable atoms and molecules : there are molecules of oxygen each consisting of two atoms, and molecules of nitrogen analogously constituted, a few molecules of carbon dioxide, each consisting of one atom of carbon and two of oxygen, a certain number of single atoms of argon, and probably small percentages of other gases. All of them form gases because of the lack of tendency to associate; the independence which they possess in consequence, together with their motion, furnish a ready understanding of their behaviour.

We now ask ourselves whether we see any way of connecting the properties of these atoms with the general idea of atomic structure which was put forward in the last lecture. How is the sun and planet conception to be connected with these tendencies to associate, or not to associate, with the formation of molecules having similar tendencies, and so on? To answer these ques-

THE NATURE OF GASES

tions fully would be to give an account of chemistry so far as is known, and that is clearly beyond our intentions. But there are certain simple rules which, though they cannot be explained, and though they are often broken in appearance, provide a most useful thread on which to string our facts. Let us go back to our unsociable atoms, numbers 2, 10, 18, 36, 54, 86. The first thing that strikes us is that there are curious connections between these numbers. If we write down the successive differences we have 2, 8, 8, 18, 18, 32. The numbers 2, 8, 18, 32 are twice the squares of 1, 2, 3 and 4. We have already seen that the difference between the various kinds of atoms is simply one of number. I have not attempted to explain the experimental and theoretical proofs of the numbers of electrons on the various atoms: they are complicated, while the result is simple and sufficient for our purpose. Since the number of the electrons on the atom, or rather the number which expresses the positive charge on its nucleus, is in itself of such unique importance, we cannot but think that there must be something underlying the curious numerical differences we have just observed. The probability is greatly increased when we consider the question from another point of view.

Chemists have long discovered and pointed out that remarkable analogies exist between the properties of different kinds of atoms. For our purpose it will be convenient to express their discoveries in terms of the numerical relations. We write down some of them in the following way. We take first the eight atoms, in order of number, which begin with helium; and put under them the next eight beginning with neon. We thus have, continuing the arrangement up to No. 20 (see Plate IV B for rough models) :—

Helium.	Lithium.	Beryllium.	Boron.	Carbon.	Nitrogen.	Oxygen.	Fluorine.
2	3	4	5	6	7	8	9
Neon.	Sodium.	Magnesium.	Aluminium.	Silicon.	Phosphorus.	Sulphur.	Chlorine.
10	11	12	13	14	15	16	17
Argon.	Potassium.	Calcium,	and so on.				
18	19	20					

We have, in fact, written down a portion of the " periodic table." It is so set out that the atoms helium, neon and argon, which so closely resemble each other in their main property of unsociability, are in the same column. It then appears that lithium, sodium and potassium, which also closely resemble each other in their properties, are in the next column, and that the same remarkable classification runs across the page. The mutual resemblances of the substances in the same column are manifested in innumerable ways : they form one of the great

THE NATURE OF GASES 77

features of chemistry. The very name "periodic table" was adopted as a description of the fact.

Now it is reasonable to suppose that the properties of an atom as manifested by its relation to any other may well be determined by some arrangement of its electrons, and especially of those which are most on the surface and are first presented to the other atom. Thus lithium, sodium and potassium probably behave alike, because they have all the same external presentment of electrons; so with carbon and silicon, with fluorine and chlorine, and so on.

Such considerations have led to the following hypothesis. Let the two electrons of helium be arranged as a pair symmetrically placed on either side of the helium nucleus. Let every succeeding atom have the same arrangement, and, in addition, a further arrangement of electrons on an outer shell. Thus lithium has two, like helium, and one as a contribution to a new outside grouping. Beryllium has two in the outside group, boron three, carbon four, nitrogen five, oxygen six and fluorine seven. We will suppose that the list of additions to this list closes with neon, and that in all atoms of higher number the inside group of two and the just completed group of eight are retained, the extra electrons taking their place in new groups. Thus, sodium, like lithium, has one in its outermost group, magnesium has two, like beryllium, and so on. Chlorine, like fluorine, has all but completed an outer shell of eight; while argon, like neon, has completed it. With potassium still another group begins; calcium has two in this newest group, and so on. The last group is not complete until it contains eighteen electrons; so chemical evidence tells us. But we need not pursue this question further, especially as it becomes more complicated.

Arguing in this way, we understand why the members of the same columns should be alike in their properties. We then ask what the particular properties of an atom have to do with the particular number of electrons there are in its outer shell, this number being the same in all members of the same column. To this question also we can find some sort of answer which we can best state in the following way. From a general consideration of the vast accumulation of chemical knowledge regarding the tendencies of atoms to form combinations, and under proper circumstances to dissolve existing combinations and form new ones, certain rules appear which are directly connected with the numbers of the

THE NATURE OF GASES 79

electrons in the outermost groups. In the first place, there is always a tendency to fill up the vacant places of an uncompleted group. Thus if chlorine had one more electron in its external group, that group would be completed in the sense that no more additions are made to it as we pass from atom to atom in the succeeding portions of the table. Consequently chlorine is on the search, so to speak, for the electron which it lacks, and may exert great powers in dragging it away from other atoms which are not holding on to it with sufficient energy. It is true that the atom's electricities thus become unevenly balanced: the extra electron gives it a negative charge. But in spite of that there is some force, we do not understand its origin, which works for the completion of the external shell of eight electrons. It is, in fact, this power that chlorine possesses of dragging to itself an electron from other atoms, and upsetting their combination in order to get it, which makes the substance so actively poisonous. In the same way, sulphur has two gaps to fill up, and its behaviour is largely governed by that fact.

On the other hand, lithium, sodium, potassium have in each case a group just in process of formation: there is so far only one electron in it. The hold upon this electron is feeble, and when a chlorine atom demands it, the electron changes hands at once. The result of the transfer is that the external group of each atom is now a completed group: the chlorine is like argon externally, and, if sodium be the other atom, it is now like neon. Both the atoms are now charged with electricity: the chlorine is negative because it has one electron in excess of its proper number, while the sodium atom is positive because it has one too few to make the balance between the positive charge on the nucleus and the negative charges of the electrons that are left. In consequence, there is an electric attraction between the two atoms: they have now formed a molecule of ordinary salt. Sodium is a soft white metal. As we shall see later, the distinguishing characteristic of the metals is their possession of one or two electrons which can be easily torn from them. In this combination the white metal and the poisonous gas have joined to make the transparent crystalline salt. It is a violent change of character; but it will not surprise us if we remember that the arrangement of the electrons on the outside of the molecule must be quite different from the arrangement on either of the atoms before they become partners,

THE NATURE OF GASES

and that the character of the atom or the molecule depends on this arrangement.

There are innumerable examples of this kind of combination. As one involving rather more complication we may take calcium fluoride, which as a crystal goes under the name of fluorspar. Here two atoms of fluorine, each lacking one electron (see the table above), join in an attack upon calcium, which has two electrons in its external group, and each of them takes one electron into its own system. The molecule therefore contains three atoms. Or, again, in alumina, which in crystalline form makes ruby or sapphire, we have two atoms of aluminium, each forced to give up the three electrons in its external group for the benefit of three oxygen atoms, each of which takes two.

Besides this give-and-take arrangement there is another method by which atoms seek to complete their external groups: they may share electrons with one another, each being capable, apparently, of counting them in its own structure, just as two houses may have the same party-wall. Thus two hydrogen atoms, each contributing one electron, combine so as to possess a group of two, as helium does, and thus the hydrogen molecule is formed. Two atoms of oxygen enter into combination, and form the oxygen molecule in which each oxygen atom is surrounded by eight electrons, of which four are held in common by both atoms. In the diamond, as we shall see, each carbon atom is surrounded by four other carbon atoms, with each of which it shares two electrons. So each atom is provided with an external shell of eight electrons, none of which it has entirely to itself. This kind of combination is generally very strong, and molecules so formed hold together well. Moreover, many molecules formed in this way are, so to speak, satisfied with their own company : there is little tendency to associate with other molecules. They tend to form gases. But on the whole the most permanent gases are those which have naturally the completed external shell—helium, neon, argon and the rest. They show, most fully developed, the gaseous properties which we have been considering as the result of the weakness of tendencies to associate and the undisputed sway of movement.

LECTURE III

THE NATURE OF LIQUIDS

THE difference between a gas and a liquid is that in the former the atoms and molecules move to and fro in an independent existence, whereas in the latter they are always in touch with one another though they are changing partners continually. In the rivalry between motion and attractive forces the motion is no longer in complete control: the attractive forces have now sufficient power to keep the general body of molecules in touch with each other, or at least so many of them so that they form a definite volume of liquid, having a surface that we can see. Yet the control of the attractive forces is not absolute: there is a continual process which we call evaporation. Suppose a bowl of water to be placed in an empty room. The molecules of the water are all in movement—vibrating, turning, shifting and changing partners all the time. But their motion is not enough to make them break away from one another, except at the surface, where the conditions are of a special nature. In consequence the molecules hold together as a body having a definite volume, and there are boundaries to that volume. Only at the surface there are breakaways: in the constant interchange of motion it will happen that some of the outlying molecules have impulses given to them which are big enough to break their connection with the molecules below, and they leave the surface for good. If this had happened to molecules within the liquid, they would have been recaptured. Thus the room in which the bowl of water has been placed will contain a gradually increasing number of water molecules flying about independently as a gas. If the room is closed, the increase will not go on for ever, because there will come a time when the number of free water molecules in the room is so great that molecules strike the surface of the water and re-enter it as fast as others leave it. The room has become saturated with water vapour. That may happen before the bowl is empty; but if the air in the room is continuously removed, carrying the water vapour with it, the water in the bowl will all evaporate in time.

The molecules that leave the surface will always be those that possess more than the

THE NATURE OF LIQUIDS 85

average amount of energy, part of which they spend in tearing themselves away from their fellows; the average energy of the main body will fall steadily as evaporation proceeds. In other words, the water becomes colder and colder. We all know this effect well. If we wave our hands when they are wet we feel the chill: we are, in fact, using somewhat excessively a process which Nature employs to cool our bodies to the proper temperature. Our bodies are called on to make good the excess of energy which the evaporating molecules have carried away with them. The rate of chilling may be increased by the use of a liquid which evaporates more rapidly than water; so, for example, the surgeon at one time used an ether spray to cause local freezing. In hot, dry countries drinking water is cooled by putting it into a bag made of porous canvas, which is hung so as to be shaded from the sun but exposed to the wind, and the hotter and drier the wind the better. In the hot Australian summer it is usual to see the bag hanging under the verandah of the house or the roof of the railway station of a country township. The water leaks through the canvas and is quickly evaporated by the passing air, so that the water which is left grows cool.

We can carry out the experiment in a very striking manner on the lecture-room table. The two bulbs shown in the figure contain water only, no air. The water is first brought to the upper bulb, and the lower is then immersed in liquid air; in two or three minutes the water is frozen, although the upper bulb has been nowhere near the liquid air. The explanation is that the water molecules which fling themselves from the surface of the water make their way down the tube and so to the lower bulb. This would happen whether or no there were any liquid air round the lower vessel; but then they would come back again, most of them at least, and return

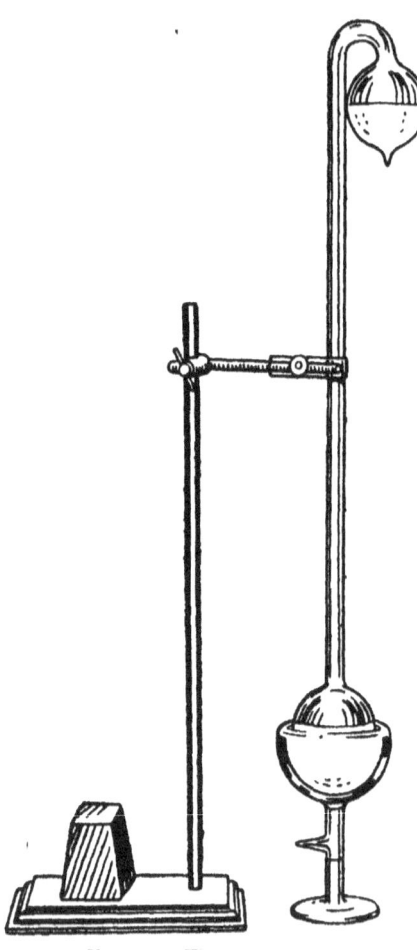

FIG. 13.—The cryophorus.
The lower bulb, which is empty, is immersed in liquid air. The upper bulb contains water which quickly freezes.

THE NATURE OF LIQUIDS 87

to the water carrying their superabundant energy with them. Thus the water would be very little cooled. If, however, the lower bulb is reduced in temperature by the liquid air, the molecules do not return. Their motion is taken away from them and they collect first as water and then as ice in the lower bulb. The water in the upper bulb is rapidly cooled, and soon frozen. The reason for removing the air from the bulbs is that it is necessary to give the water molecules a clear road, so that the evaporation may take place quickly. If the operation were too slow, heat would leak in from the outside air at such a rate that the freezing would not take place. The presence of the air does not stop the energetic molecules from leaving the surface, but it hampers their subsequent movements, reducing the action to the process of diffusion which we have already considered.

When a liquid boils, the temperature has been raised to such a pitch that the evaporating molecules are sufficient in number and speed to lift off the air from the surface of the liquid and push it back *en masse*. It is no longer the case that the individual molecules have to thread their way through a crowd. The whole process is so strikingly different in appearance from that of evaporation that the essential similarity is apt to be overlooked. The temperature at which a liquid boils depends on the pressure which the evaporating molecules have to overcome : at the top of Mount Blanc boiling water is 27° F. cooler than it is at the base.

The heat that is wanted if a liquid is to be evaporated is a measure of the energy required to tear the molecules away from one another. Perhaps that does not impress the mind with a sense of the importance of these forces, which, though individually minute, are so powerful in the gross. We may, however, remind ourselves of the heat required to convert water into steam and of the amount of work that the steam can do. The forces are manifested to us more directly in every hanging drop of water or other liquid. The molecules are clinging to one another like bees in a swarm. The links with which the molecules of the last layer are attached to the surface from which the drop is hanging are carrying the whole weight of the drop. Again the impression of the magnitude and importance of the forces is not fairly conveyed by this simple effect; but the experiment can be developed into a more impressive form. Here is a bent glass tube containing water and no air. The water is made to

THE NATURE OF LIQUIDS

fill one limb entirely; if a little bubble of air is to be found in it, it must be made to pass over into the other by holding the tube in a suitable position and gently tapping it on the table. When this has been done, the tube can be held so that the level of the free end of the water column is far below the level of the other, where it is clinging to the end of the glass tube. The weight of the excess column on one side is all borne by the attachment of the water molecules to the glass tube at

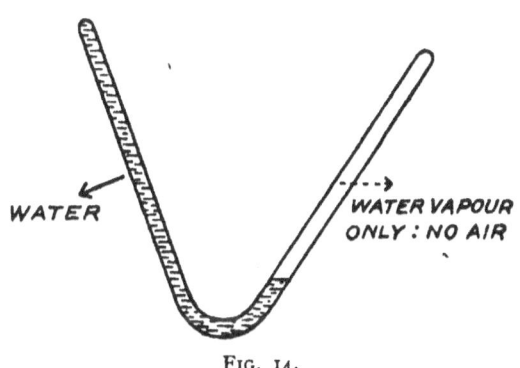

FIG. 14.

the other side, and of other water molecules to them. In fact, we have a drop of water about a foot long. We cannot make a drop of this length hang from a finger; for the reason that the water can break away by changing its shape. If that is prevented, as it is in the glass tube, the magnitude of these molecular forces is more obvious. When we try to stretch a bar of iron, the great difficulty makes us realise the magnitude of the forces that keep the molecules of solid iron together; we are apt to think that it is easy to stretch a mass of water, but it is not so. It is easy to make the water change its shape, but not to pull a layer of molecules directly away from another with which it is in contact. Water is, in reality, just as hard to stretch as to compress.

We may here make a little digression from our main line of argument, because we come across a curious effect while we handle this bent tube. If the tube is tilted so that the water runs along the tube and is brought up sharply at one end, the sound of a blow is heard, as of two hard substances striking one another; the blow is felt by the hand that holds the tube. The effect is sometimes described as an example of water hammer; the explanation is simple enough. There is no air in the tube, and the water strikes the end of the tube as if it were a rigid body; and indeed it behaves as such because it is as incompressible. It is necessary to be very careful in the handling of the tubes, because it is so easy to knock out an end : it is just as if we struck a glass vessel with a hammer. A very curious, and as it happens very serious, example of this effect has manifested itself of recent years in the wearing away of the propellers of ships that are driven by rapidly turning screws. The illustration shows

PLATE IX.

A

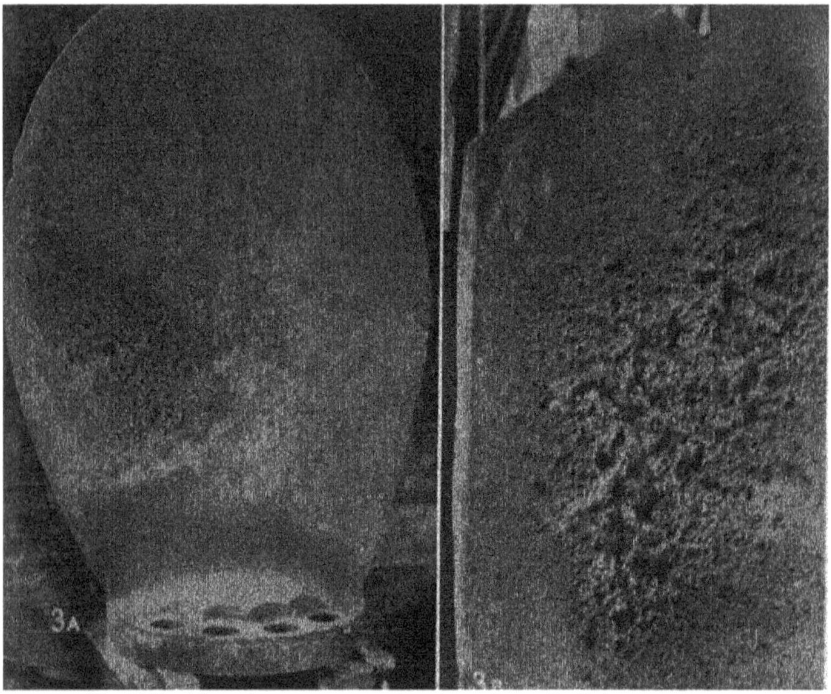

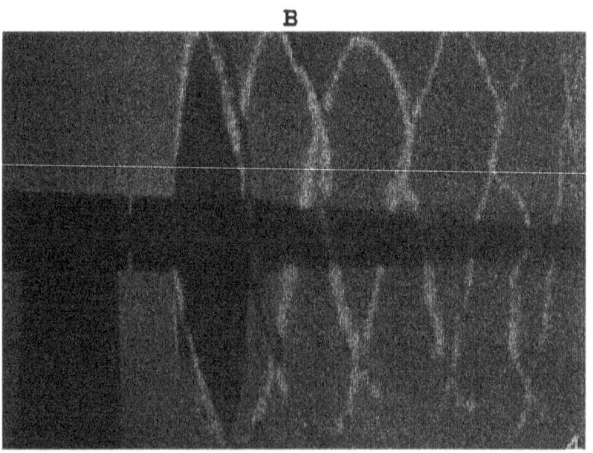

The right-hand figure shows erosion in a portion of an early propeller blade of the "Mauretania." Notice the small bite in the edge of the blade shown in full in the left-hand figure.

B

Photograph of the cavitations formed by a propeller in the experimental tank of the Parsons Marine Steam Turbine Co. The propeller is the disc-shaped object at the left centre of the photograph. There are three blades on it, and each is leaving a corkscrew line of bubbles in the water which goes past the blade. We can see where the spirals begin at the screw.

[Reproduced by courtesy of the Manganese Bronze and Brass Co., Ltd.

THE NATURE OF LIQUIDS 91

the erosion in a propeller blade of the *Mauretania* (Plate IX A). The effect first appeared when the adoption of the Parsons steam turbine increased the rate of revolution of the screw and boats began to move faster, and it was at first the cause of great loss, financial and otherwise. The explanation was found in the fact that the steamship was advancing so fast and the screws were revolving so rapidly that the water could not fill up entirely the holes that the blades left behind them. The illustration shows the cavities as they are formed in a model tank in the Turbinia Works at Newcastle (Plate IX B). They are arranged in spirals; we can trace in the figure the spiral belonging to each of the propeller blades.

Now these cavities close up under the pressure of the surrounding water, and since there is no air in them, the sides of the cavity strike one another as hard and smartly, when they come together, as the water in our tube could be made to strike the glass. If part of the propeller blade forms part of a cavity wall, the blow may be so great as to tear away pieces of the metal. It has cost much labour to arrive at the full explanation and to provide a cure: propeller blades are now made of an alloy specially designed to withstand erosion, and at the same time the design of the blade has been improved. A very striking experiment made in the course of these researches is illustrated in Fig. 15. The strong metal vessel shown in the centre of the figure is filled with water and allowed to fall to the bottom of a tank, also full of water, where its motion is suddenly stopped. The momentum of the water in the cone aided by that of the heavy weight W is sufficient to make the water carry on its motion and leave a cavity at the top of the cone at V. This fills up again immediately afterwards, on account of the pressure of the surrounding water, and as it does so the water in the cone, increasing its velocity as it rushes up into the narrowing space, strikes the top of the cavity so hard that it punches a hole in the brass plate inserted at P.

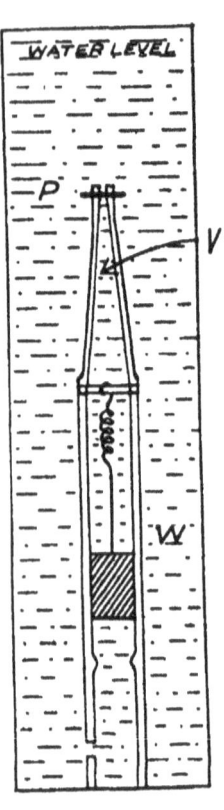

FIG. 15.—Parsons' water hammer.

The collapsing of the cavities formed by the screw makes quite a noise in the water, so that a ship can be heard at great distances by the use of an underwater receiver of sound.

Many of my audience will be familiar with a

THE NATURE OF LIQUIDS

less serious example of the blow that a mass of water can give because of its inelasticity: it hurts considerably if one dives from any height and does not make a proper entry into the water!

Since the molecules of a liquid all try to draw together under their united attractions, they will bunch themselves together into a sphere if they are allowed to do so, and this happens obviously when mercury is dropped upon the table and

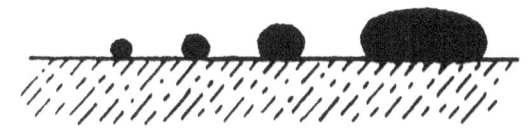

DROPS OF MERCURY ON A TABLE
FIG. 16.
The small drops are almost perfect spheres. The large drops are flattened out.

breaks up into round drops which run about as if they were round and hard. Water will do the same thing if it does not wet the table: generally it does wet the solid on which it rests, but we see many exceptions, as, for example, when it is spilt on a dusty surface. What wetting means and implies we have yet to consider: it is a very important part of our subject. Gravitation also interferes with the tendency of a liquid to gather into spheres. When the drops of mercury are very small they look perfectly round, but larger masses are more like thick discs with rounded edges. If we seek for good examples of the formation of spheres by the general attraction of the molecules for one another, we must contrive to avoid the influences both of wetting and gravitation. The small drops of mercury are a successful illustration. Another is to be found in the manufacture of lead shot. The molten lead is allowed to fall in a shower from the top of the shot tower, and gathers into round drops as it falls, just as the rain does.

Perhaps it seems as if this were inconsistent with what has gone before : gravitation has not been avoided and is indeed in full action, yet the drops are formed. But the evil effect of gravitation is indirect; it is the resistance to gravity which spoils the formation of spheres. In the case of the large drops of mercury, the flattening is due, not to gravitation directly, but to the upward pressure of the table, which is resisting gravitation. When the drops of lead arrive at the bottom of the tower they fall into water, which freezes them in the shape they have acquired.

Here is an experiment to illustrate our point. The dark-looking liquid, ortho-toluidine, does not mix with water, or, in other words, water does

PLATE X.

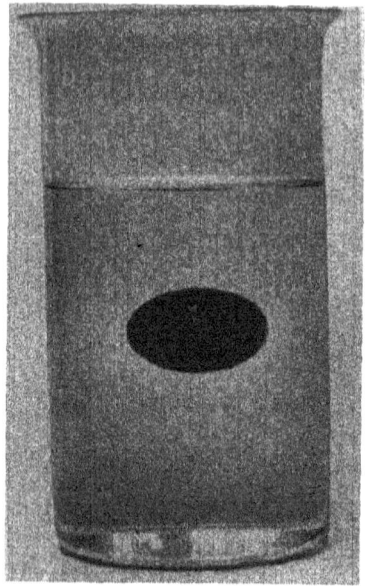 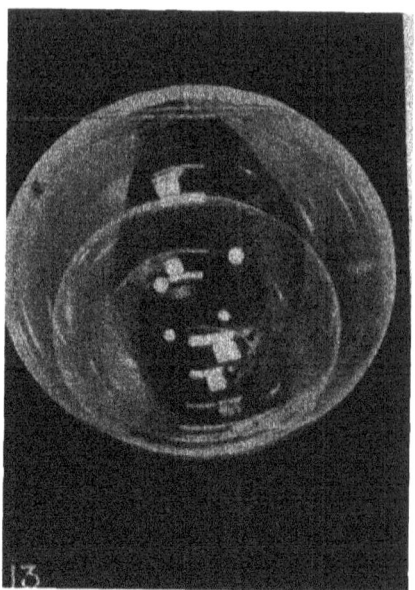

A **B**

A. A large drop of liquid orthotoluidine floating in water on a layer of brine.
B. One bubble rests inside another, but as in Fig. 21 and for the same reason the two do not coalesce.

THE NATURE OF LIQUIDS

not "wet" it, and its density is such that it floats conveniently in a layer of pure water riding on a layer of salt water (Plate X A). It is, even when spherical, supported at all points by the surrounding water: it is not held up at one point only, as a mercury drop would have to be were it a sphere resting on a hard surface. In the circumstances of our experiment neither wetting nor gravitation has any influence, and a large drop is formed, as we see: it is perhaps a couple of inches in diameter. If it is pulled about by a glass rod it sluggishly recovers itself; or, after wobbling heavily through a variety of strange shapes, may break into smaller spheres. When the rod is pressed gently against the sphere it makes a depression or dimple on the surface; the toluidine's effort to form a spherical drop is for the moment interfered with, but it adapts itself as well as possible to the circumstances. So also if we float some solid body—an iron ball, let us say—on the surface of mercury, a dimple is formed; the surface of the mercury near the ball has the form shown in the figure. If we look at the form of the mercury surface close to the wall of the containing vessel, we see the same outline.

It is different when the liquid wets the wall of the vessel which holds it or of the body which floats in it. If we put clean water into a clean glass vessel, we see the water heaping itself against the side. This is a more complicated effect than the other; evidently there are attractive forces between the glass and the water.

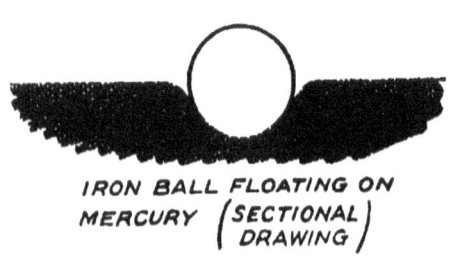

Fig 17.—Iron ball floating on mercury (sectional drawing).

If a glass plate is forced down into a dish full of mercury and made to touch the bottom so that the mercury is squeezed out and none remains between the plate and the bottom of the dish, it will stay where it is put, and indeed great force is required to remove it. The explanation is simple and in accordance with the principles which we have been considering. If the plate is to rise, the mercury must be made to get under it again, otherwise the plate cannot rise far, because if there is not a vacuum under the plate there is at most only a little air, which would fall

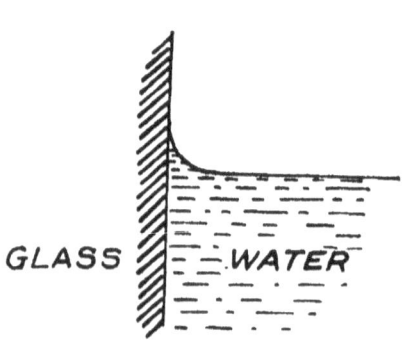

Fig. 18.—Water heaped up against glass wall which it wets.

THE NATURE OF LIQUIDS

rapidly in pressure if the plate were raised. As the pressure on the top of the plate is more than that of the atmosphere, the downward forces on the plate are greater than those which try to lift it. At the edge of the plate the form of the mercury surface is as shown in the figure: the mercury refuses to allow itself to be drawn out into a thin sheet between the plate and the bottom of the vessel.

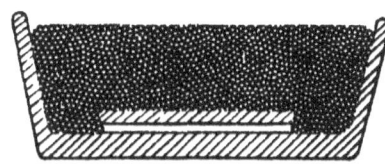

Fig. 19.—Glass plate at bottom of dish containing mercury. The plate is shown slightly lifted from the bottom, in order to illustrate the refusal of the mercury to enter the vacuum so made.

A drop of fluid which tries to draw itself together into a sphere looks as if it were being held in an elastic bag. The atoms of mercury in the surface are not quite in the same circumstances as those in the interior, because they are exposed on one side, but it is only in this sense that there is a surface film. We use the idea of a surface film, nevertheless, finding it a convenient term; and we speak of its tendency to contract and of its tension. Sometimes, however, there is a real film on the surface which is different in composition from the liquid of the interior, and then we find many strange and beautiful consequences. The example most familiar to us is, no doubt, that of the soap bubble. We put into the water a little soap, and at once we find it easy to churn the soapy water into a pile of froth or blow it out into bubbles. What has the soap to do with this effect? The answer is to be found in the properties of the soap molecule. It is of very curious shape, many times as long as it is broad; and it is made up of a chain of carbon atoms fringed along its length with hydrogens, and ending, at one end, in a little bunch of three hydrogen atoms, at the other in a little group consisting of oxygen and sodium. The former of these bunches is very self-contained: its attractions for other atoms and molecules are small. But the latter is by no means so unsociable: it is an active group tending to enter into association with others, and especially it has a strong desire to join up with molecules of water, for which reason the soap dissolves in the water. Because, however, it is only one end of the chain which is very active in this respect—the other end and the sides of the chain behave differently—the soap molecules are apt to stay on the outer fringe of the water if they come there in the course of their wanderings. In this way a real film forms on the surface of the water, consisting of soap molecules standing on end, so to speak,

THE NATURE OF LIQUIDS

one end rooted in the water, and the other exposed to the air. They are packed together side by side like the corn in a field, or the pile on a piece of velvet. They are not as free, however, as the hairs of the pile: they are tied together side by side, because there is some force of attraction between them when so laid alongside. We find that effect displayed under other circumstances, as we shall see later. Thus they form a sort of chain mail over the surface of the water: a real envelope. The sheet can be stretched in the sense that if it has to be extended other long molecules will come out of the body of the liquid and take their place with the rest.

The soap bubble is a thin-walled sphere of solution bounded within and without by the soap films; it holds together so well because the films are there. It shrinks if the air within it is allowed to escape: evidently the long molecules would gather together with the water molecules as closely as possible. But there must be an outside, of course, and where both kinds of molecules are present it is the long chain molecules that form the outside layer. A very simple experiment will illustrate still further the tendency to shrink. A wire ring is dipped into some soap solution, and when lifted out carries a soap film stretched across it. In the film floats a ring of fine cotton which was attached to the wire ring before the latter was put into the solution. If the film inside the cotton loop is burst by touching it with a hot needle, the loop flies instantly into the form of a perfect circle, as the figure shows. It is clear that the whole film is under tension and is trying to contract.

A very curious feature of the soap bubble is its reluctance to join up with another bubble. If we blow a bubble on a ring (see Fig. 21), we may take a second bubble and knock it against the first with force, one would think, enough to break them. But the bubbles bounce from one another like india-rubber balloons. Perhaps the explanation lies in the fact that in both cases the outer layer consists of those ends of the molecules which, as we saw before, have very little tendency to associate with other molecules or parts of molecules. There is no tendency for

FIG. 20.
A loop of very fine cotton is floated on the soap film, and the part of the film inside the loop is touched with a hot needle. Instantly the loop flies into a perfect circle. (By courtesy of Prof. C. V. Boys.)

THE NATURE OF LIQUIDS

the one bubble to coalesce with the other when the two are pressed together, because the parts that come first into contact do not attract each other. This is very clearly seen in another of the wonderful experiments of C. V. Boys.* A bubble is blown on a ring held in a stand (Fig. 21A).

FIG. 21.—Two bubbles in collision.

The two bubbles are pressing one another, and may be rubbed on one another, but do not coalesce, because their liquids do not mix; it is only the inactive ends of chain molecules that come into contact. (By courtesy of Prof. C. V. Boys.)

A small ring carrying a tiny weight is attached to the under part of the bubble as shown. A glass pipe is charged with solution and pushed through the top of the bubble; when blown, a second bubble appears within the first, and when it has attained a suitable size is released by a skilful twist of the pipe. The inner bubble falls gently to rest on the lower part of the outer, which it touches along a ring, not at the bottom point. This is

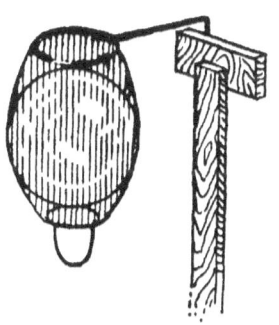

FIG. 21A.

* " Soap Bubbles and the Forces which Mould Them," C. V. Boys.

intentional, and was the purpose for which the weight was attached to the outer bubble. The two do not tend to coalesce, although in contact all along a line, no doubt because they are presenting to one another surfaces composed of the inactive or unsociable ends of the chains. If the outer bubble had not been pulled out of shape, the inner and outer would have touched each other at their lowest points. Now there is generally a drop of solution at the lowest point of the inner bubble. When this comes into contact with the outer, the bubbles generally coalesce. The drop of solution in some way forms a bridge between the two. If the glass pipe be pushed through the outer and made to touch the bottom point of the inner, and so drain it, the weight hanging from the outer may be peeled off, and now the two can touch each other at this lowest point without disaster (Plate X B).

The frothing of liquids is often caused by the presence of molecules which have the same property of forming a skin over the surface. When the foam gathers on a brook it is due to the presence of such molecules as those of the various saponins, chain-like formations which are found in many plants and trees. So also the

THE NATURE OF LIQUIDS

foam that gathers on the shore is believed to b
due to the presence of similar molecules forme
in the sea-weeds.

We have learnt much about the form of thes
long-chain molecules within recent years. I
particular we are indebted to the late Lor
Rayleigh, to Devaux in France, to Langmuir i
America, to Hardy and to Adam in England fo
the examination of what happens when oils ar
allowed to spread on water surfaces. We ca
repeat one or two of the experiments in order t
get an idea of the magnitude of the effects c
which we are speaking. We take a clean wate
surface, that is to say, a surface free from an
contamination by oil or grease. It is convenien
to attach a rubber tube to the tap, and let th
free end of the tube lie at the bottom of a basi
so that the water wells up and overflows th
edges, carrying away any dirt that has settled o
its surface. We now spread on the water a thi
dusting of talc powder or anything else that i
convenient. Next we take a fine drawn glas
point or needle and dip it into oil—olive oil wil
do—and then, after wiping nearly all the oil off
dip the point of the slightly greasy needle int
the water surface. Instantly a circle is cleare
round the needle (Plate XI A). It appears tha

the long molecules range themselves side by side on the surface as before; to the soap bubble they came from within, now we apply them from without. Each molecule hastens to root itself in the water by its active end, and stands upright, as if it were a water plant rooted and growing in the water. In the end all the molecules are successful, and a thin sheet, one molecule thick, covers the surface of the water; its thickness is of the order of a ten-millionth of an inch. By measuring the weight of the oil that has been placed on the water—a difficult task, since it is so small—and the area covered, it is possible to find a measure of the thickness of the film. This is, in fact, the method that has been followed by the workers mentioned. More recently it has been possible to apply a new method, based on the use of X-rays, to the exact measurement of the same quantity, and I hope to show you presently how this is done. On the results of the earlier work it was possible to assert that the thickness of the layer was such as would be expected if it were one molecule thick; and the argument was greatly strengthened by the fact that when different substances, known by chemists to be chain molecules of different length, were placed upon the water, the thickness varied with the length, as it ought to do.

PLATE XI.

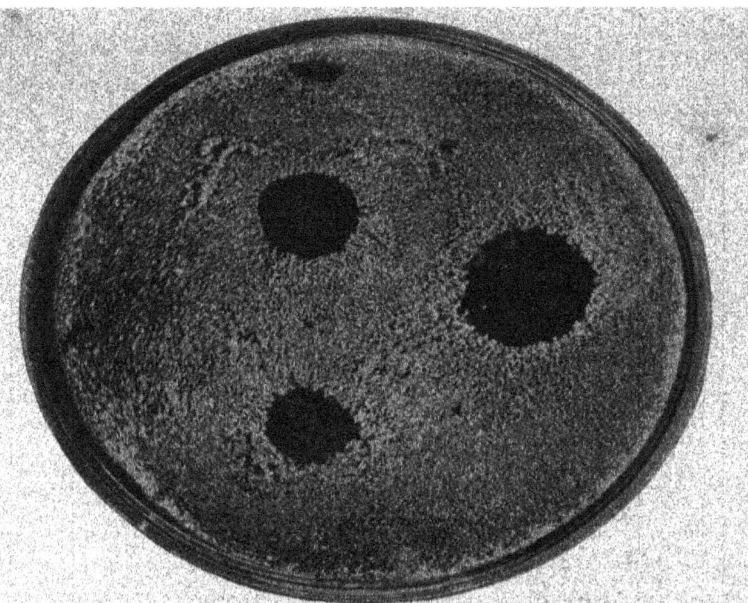

A. Circles cleared by minute drops of oil.

B. The camphor boat.
A small piece of camphor is fastened at the stern of a very light boat, and as it dissolves in the water the solution forms a film on the surface. It is so eager to do so that it drives the boat away so as to make room for itself. If a little oil is put on the water and makes a film all over it, the boat stops. If the oil partly covers the water, the boat stops as soon as the ruler which is held by the operator in the picture is pushed so far forward that the oil covers the surface left to it.

THE NATURE OF LIQUIDS

If the drop of oil is small enough, and the dust is finely scattered, the cleared spot is exactly circular. If we prick the water surface somewhere else, another circle is formed. Each circle is totally unaffected by the presence of others. This was relied on by Devaux to show that the action of each drop was concerned only with the surface round it over which the oil was spread: it was not a general effect on the body of the liquid. It was just what one would expect if the drop of oil had spread out until it was drawn down to a certain thickness and could then spread no further. By putting on a larger drop, we can see that larger spaces are cleared. We may, for example, pour a few drops into a large bath, and clear the whole surface. When the dust layer on the surface of the water is broken up into little patches by several applications of minute drops, in different places, and when the surface is not covered all over with the oil film, we can observe the quickness of the spreading by touching the surface with the oiled needle at some little distance from a floating patch, and watching how suddenly the patch is hurried away from the spot. The impulses that are given in this way are the cause of the lively movements of camphor fragments when they are dropped on the surface of the water, an old experiment. As the camphor dissolves, the solution shoots over the surface in a film, and the camphor itself recoils like a gun when it is fired, or a rocket when the heated gases stream from its tail. Sometimes the fragments dart to and fro and sometimes spin round merrily. A tiny boat can be made to sail about on the water by fastening a little piece of camphor on its stern in such a way as to touch the water (Plate XI B). When a number of camphor boats and pieces of camphor are all on the move, it is quaint to see how suddenly it all goes dead when a little oil is poured on the water. The oil film has covered the water in an instant, and the dissolved camphor no longer spreads over the surface.

We have all heard of the stilling of the waves by pouring oil upon the sea. We can watch the effect by making a series of waves run along the long tank which Lord Rayleigh once used here for the same purpose; a vacuum cleaner serves to provide the wind, and you see there is quite a heavy storm on the water (Plate XII A, B). It is magically stilled if a few drops of oil are allowed to fall in the centre of the storm; after a few moments the oil sheet is blown to the end of the tank and the waves rise once more. We can repeat the experiment again and again. We must suppose

PLATE XII.

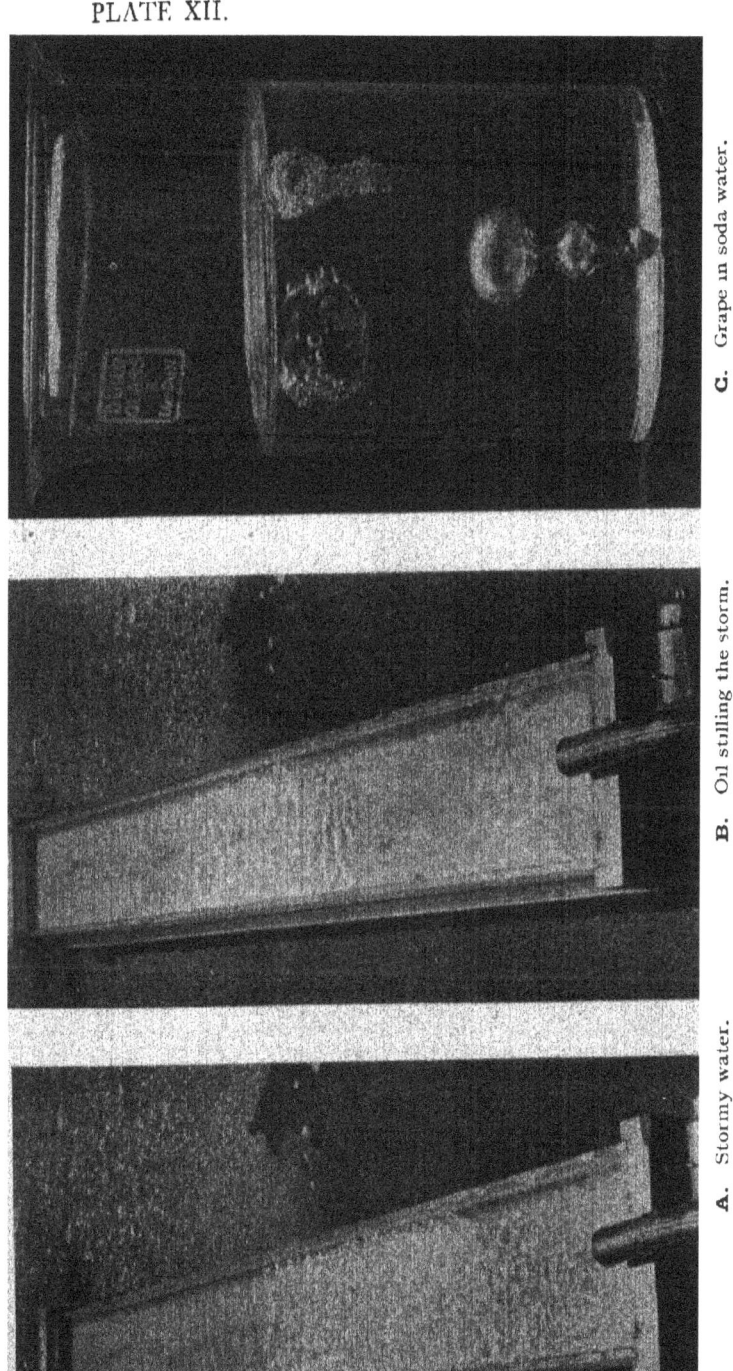

A. Stormy water. **B.** Oil stilling the storm. **C.** Grape in soda water.

A and B. The blower raises a storm and the waves run along the tank. A drop of oil stills the waves at once, and the water surface becomes level. Notice the blank space in B. After a while, the oil is blown to the end of the tank, and then the waves rise again. The photographs have been retouched so as to bring out the reflection of the light by the waves.
C. The grape and the greasy glass sinker are carried to the top by bubbles; the clean glass sinker has no bubbles and stays at the bottom.

THE NATURE OF LIQUIDS 107

in this case that the wind has no "bite" on the water. The latter is covered, as we know, with a film of oil, the top surface of which is formed of the inactive ends of the long-chain molecules; and it may well be that the molecules of the air when they strike it recoil as from a smooth surface. A rough surface would be driven forward by the impacts of the air molecules—rough, that is to say, in the sense that the spaces between the exposed molecules are of the same size as the molecules that strike. But if the surface of the oil film is very smooth and has little tendency to hold on to any molecules that strike it, the air cannot push it and make it rise in little waves which afterwards grow to great ones. So the oil stills the waves by stopping the action of the wind, and the motion of the waves dies out in their own friction.

We now come to the problem of the "wetting" of a surface. We know, for example, that a clean glass surface is wetted by water, but not when it is smeared with grease, even if the film is almost invisible. The water molecules clearly refuse to associate with the molecules of the grease. That is not surprising, perhaps, because we have seen that in some cases at least the long molecules that make the fats and oils present to the outside their inactive ends, which have very little attraction for the water molecules. So water spilt on a greasy surface gathers into drops, just as mercury when it is spilt on the table; the form of the water is due to the general attraction of its molecules for one another. An oiled needle can be gently laid on water without sinking more than to make a depression in the surface, just as if there were a skin on the water which gave slightly under the weight. Still more striking, perhaps, is the floating of a greased wire sieve (Fig. 22). The sieve is dipped in melted paraffin wax, shaken so as to clear the pores, and allowed to dry; it is well not to touch it with the fingers. It will float readily and carry quite a lot of cargo, as Boys showed at the Christmas Lectures many years ago. Or it may be filled with water; but the water must not be poured in roughly, it must be allowed to flow in gently on to a piece of paper which can afterwards be removed. To show that the pores are quite

FIG. 22.—Greased sieve. (By courtesy of Prof. C. V. Boys.)

THE NATURE OF LIQUIDS 109

open we can give the sieve a sharp movement, when the water film gives way and the water falls in a heavy shower on the floor.

When soda water is poured out into a clean, smooth tumbler, very few bubbles come to the surface; but if the surface of the tumbler is at all dirty or rough we may see streams of bubbles rising. There is a beautiful old experiment which illustrates this effect, that of "the grape and champagne." We must use soda water instead of champagne. A grape is not wetted by water, and so when it is put into the tumbler it sinks to the bottom of the soda water, where it collects bubbles at a great rate (Plate XII C). Soon it is covered over with a sheet of bubbles that look like seed-pearls, and these bring it by their buoyancy to the surface. The grape is not much heavier than the water, and does not require much to lift it. At the surface the grape parts with some of its bubbles, which burst into the open air, and this goes on until it sinks again, only to collect a few more bubbles and once more be made buoyant. The process will repeat itself continually for many minutes until the soda water is "dead."

It is interesting to put in two glass beads instead of the grape. They have been cleaned:

washing with soap and water is efficient. No bubbles form on them and they stay at the bottom. We take one of them out, rub it over with a greasy finger, and now it behaves like the grape, collecting bubbles, rising, parting with some of them, falling, and so on.

We must realise that when a bubble of carbonic acid gas forms in the soda water the particles of the gas have to collect and push back the water all round. Now the water molecules are holding on to each other tightly, and resist being torn asunder. For this reason we do not see the bubbles forming in the middle of the water. At the edge, when the glass is clean, the water wets the glass, or, in other words, the water molecules are clinging to the glass even harder than they cling to one another. Bubbles cannot under those circumstances form here either, for they would have to tear away the molecules from the glass. But it is different if the surface is greasy and the molecules are not really holding on to the glass—merely pressed against it by the pressure of the rest of the water which is behind them. In that case the gas bubbles find somewhere to grow, and quickly increase in size. It is easier to push back the surrounding water when the bubbles have grown somewhat. One of the most beautiful ways of showing that is by another of Boys' soap-bubble experiments. Two bubbles of different sizes are blown on the two ends of the same tube; when they are allowed, through the opening of a tap, to communicate with one another, the little bulb blows out the big one and disappears. Of the mass of bubbles in the soda water which lie side by side on the wall or the grape, the larger ones tend to take up the smaller, and all of them to amalgamate.

The little streams of bubbles that we sometimes see rising from definite points on the surface of the tumbler are due to some irregularity in the glass—a tiny protuberance, perhaps—on which, if a bubble tends to form, it already is past the earliest stages of small diameters.

This tendency of bodies under water to collect bubbles and rise to the surface has of recent years become the basis of a great metallurgical industry. Various metal ores when crushed into powder form a mixture of particles of rock material, such as quartz and various silicates, and of metallic sulphides. It is found possible to treat the mixture so as to cover the particles containing metal with a thin oil film, which is not wetted by water, while at the same time the particles of rock are still clean and the water wets them. The mass is then churned up into a froth. All the metal-bearing particles are made buoyant by the adherence of bubbles and rise to the top in a thick frothy scum; the rest of the ore stays at the bottom of the vat, and the two parts are easily separated.

There is one other experiment which will help to illustrate these principles. We know that water heaps itself up against the side of a clean glass vessel which contains it. The molecules cling to the glass, and as it were climb up the wall on each other's shoulders in their eagerness to affix themselves thereto. If we dip two glass plates side by side in the water, the water rises higher to the space between them than it does outside. Those that are climbing one wall now help those that are climbing the other. The effect is spoken of as being due to "capillary" action," the name being given to it because it is so marked in the case of a fine or "capillary" tube. The water in the fine bore is lifted up to a great height, one inch in the case of a tube of $\frac{1}{20}$ inch diameter. If we float a small hollow glass ball on the surface of the water, the water rises up the sides of the ball. If two floating balls are made to approach each other, they will, when within a short distance—perhaps half an

THE NATURE OF LIQUIDS

inch—of each other, move together, at the end quite violently. We shall understand that if we consider the diagram in Fig. 23. Two glass balls are floating in the water. The pressure at Q is less than the pressure at the level of the dotted line, because Q is at a higher level in the water. The pressure at the level of the dotted

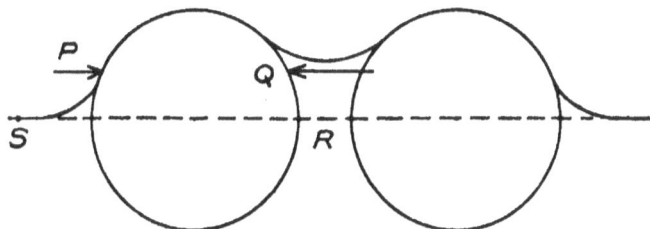

FIG. 23.—Two hollow glass balls floating in mercury.

The pressure at Q is less than the pressure at R because it is at a higher level in the water. The pressure at R is the same as at S, because R and S are on the same level. The pressure at S is that of the atmosphere which is the same as the pressure at P. Hence the pressure at P is greater than the pressure at Q, and the one glass ball is forced towards the other.

line is the pressure of the atmosphere, because the line continues the level of the water without. So the two pressures marked P, both sensibly equal to the pressure of the atmosphere, overcome the two pressures marked Q and drive the balls together.

If we float on the water two balls made of paraffin, or two glass balls coated with paraffin, the two attract each other as the clean glass balls did, though the action is somewhat different.

As the figure shows, the balls combine in making a dimple in the water, and again if we study the forces acting on the balls we find that the pressures

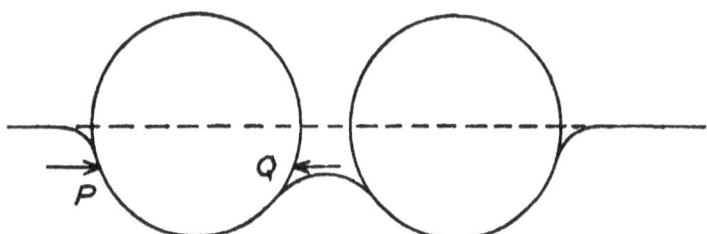

FIG. 24.—Two greased glass balls floating on water.

The pressure at P is greater than that of the atmosphere and therefore than that of Q, and the balls are forced together.

are such as to force the balls together. But the clean glass balls avoid the paraffin balls. This action is a little more complicated, but it can be followed from the figure, which shows the

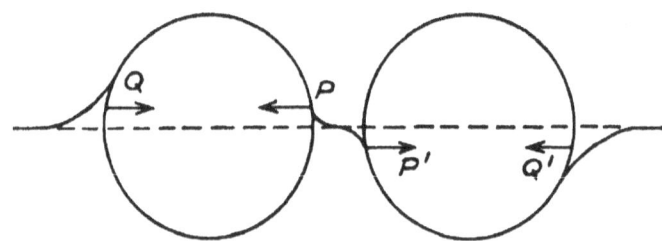

FIG. 25.

The left-hand ball is wetted by the water; the right-hand ball is greased and is not wetted. The pressure at P is greater than that at Q, and at P' greater than at Q'. Thus the balls are forced apart.

forces that are in action. When the vessel containing the water is clean, and the water is heaped up against the sides, the clean glass balls are attracted to the side, just as they are attracted

THE NATURE OF LIQUIDS 115

by each other. On the other hand, the paraffin balls avoid the side of the vessel. If now we carefully fill up the vessel with water until it tends to brim over, so that the edge of the water no longer curls up against the side, but curls down towards the edge of the vessel, the clean balls leave for the middle and the paraffin balls come to the side and stay there.

All these facts which we have been considering are illustrations of the one principle on which the formation of a liquid depends, namely, the strength of the attractions between the atoms and the molecules which are strong enough to keep them in constant association with each other, though they are not so strong as to bind them together into a rigid, solid body. And it is important to remember that molecule attaches itself to molecule at special points; one part of a molecule may be able to exert a strong hold on a special part of another. Presented differently to each other, there may be little or no tendency for the two to join together.

LECTURE IV

THE NATURE OF CRYSTALS: DIAMOND

WE have seen that when the effects of movement overcome the forces of mutual attraction, the atoms and molecules have an independent existence and form a gas; and, further, that when the attractive forces are somewhat stronger or the effects of movement are somewhat less, the molecules may cling together and form a liquid. In this state we suppose that the connections between the molecules are loose enough to allow a molecule to change its position and its partners with ease. We have now to consider a final state in which the attractive forces have quite the upper hand. The bonds between the molecules are more numerous, and it may be stronger: each molecule is tied to its neighbours at more than one point of its structure, so that it is riveted into its place, and in this way the *solid* is formed.

Molecules differ very much from one another in their form and in the forces which they exert

THE NATURE OF CRYSTALS

on one another. When the forces are strong, much movement is required to prevent them from binding the molecules into the solid: in other words, the melting point is comparatively high. Substances like diamond or tungsten, of which the filaments of electric lamps are made, are so tightly bound together that they must be raised to temperatures of several thousands of degrees centigrade before the molecules are forced to release their hold. Such substances as butter or naphthalene barely remain solid at ordinary temperatures; others, again, like carbon dioxide, still more oxygen or hydrogen, must be greatly reduced in temperature before solidification takes place. It is all a matter of the balance between the two opposing agencies, motion and mutual attraction, and it is easy to realise that the melting points of substances may differ very widely from each other.

Furthermore, a molecule is not to be thought of as a body of vague and uncertain form exerting a loosely directed attraction on its neighbours. When two molecules are brought together they may or may not draw tightly together: everything will depend on the way they are presented to each other. Each molecule has a definite shape or outline, we may say; though in using these words we must remember that their meaning will require careful consideration when we look more closely into the matter. The molecules join together as if there were definite points of attachment on each, and the junction implied that the proper points were brought together. The action between them is not usually to be compared to the general attraction between two oppositely electrified bodies, but rather to the riveting together of two parts of a mechanical structure, such as two parts of an iron bridge. Just as in the latter case the parts must be brought into the proper relative positions so that the rivets can be dropped into their places, so we find two molecules of a solid substance tend to arrange themselves so that certain parts of one are fastened with considerable rigidity to the proper corresponding parts of the other. There may be more than one way in which molecules can be joined up, and in consequence different structures may be formed out of the same molecules; for example, there are different forms of sulphur, of quartz and of many other things. It often happens that one mode of arrangement is adopted at one temperature, and a different mode at another temperature.

The consequence is that when the molecule

THE NATURE OF CRYSTALS 119

contains many atoms, and is, therefore, probably of complicated structure and curious form, the solid that is formed by their union is of a lace-like formation in space. We may compare it to a bridge formed of iron struts and stays; which is a very empty structure, because each member is peculiar in form, generally long and narrow, and is attached to the neighbouring members at definite points. Most organic substances, like naphthalene, or one of the solid paraffins, have such a complicated character, and the emptiness of the structure makes for a low density. Few organic substances are much heavier than water. When the molecules are less complicated, less irregular in outline, they may pack together more closely; if the molecule contains one or two atoms only, like the molecule of ruby, or iron pyrites, still more if it contains but one atom, atom and molecule being then equivalent terms, as in the case of gold or iron, then the packing may be very close, and we have relatively heavy substances.

The infinite variety in the properties of the solid materials we find in the world is really the expression of the infinite variety of the ways in which the atoms and molecules can be tied together, and of the strength of those ties. We shall never thoroughly understand the materials that we put to use every day, nor grasp their design, until we have found out at least the arrangement of the atoms and molecules in the solid, and are able to test the strength and other characteristics of the forces that hold them together.

Now, within the last few years the discovery of the X-rays has provided means by which we can look far down into the structure of solid bodies, and observe in detail the design of their composition. We have advanced a whole stage towards our ideal purpose—that is to say, towards the position from which we can see why a material composed of such and such atoms has such and such characteristics, density, strength, elasticity, conductivity for heat or electricity, and so on; or, in other words, reacts in such and such ways to electricity or magnetism, or mechanical forces, or light or heat. How far our new powers will carry us, we do not yet know; but it is certain that they will take us far and give us a new insight into all the ways in which material things or structures are handled, consciously or unconsciously, it may be in some industrial process, or it may be in some action of a living organism.

The new process is especially applicable to the

THE NATURE OF CRYSTALS

solid, and I hope to describe it in this and the following lectures, which deal especially with the solid state. It depends on the combined use of crystals and X-rays, and we must give a little consideration to each of these subjects. Let us take the crystal first.

Imagine a slowly cooling liquid to reach the stage of which I have already spoken, when the heat motions have decayed so far that the molecules or atoms begin to attach themselves rigidly together. They will lay themselves side by side, so arranged that the attractions of various points on the one for various points on the other are satisfied as far as possible. We can imagine two molecules, already tied together at one point, to swing about each other with diminishing movements until at last a second tie is made, quite suddenly, perhaps. Then it may be that a third tie is quickly made in the case of each molecule, linking it to the other of the two, or to a third; and so it becomes locked into position. Thus, as the liquid cools, molecule after molecule will take its place with others already locked together, and the solid grows.

Or it may be that a solid substance forms out of a solution in which it has been dissolved. The solution evaporates and the molecules meet each other more often, so that their association is encouraged. When the liquid has entirely disappeared, the substance is all solid. If the evaporation has been slow, the molecules as they wander on their way through the solution come to places where already a few molecules have tied themselves together, and join up with them, quietly and deliberately arranging themselves before they finally settle down, or refusing to take their places before they are presented to each other in the right way.

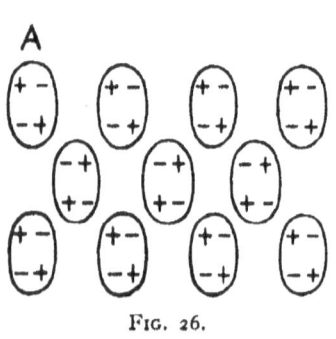

Fig. 26.

We can well imagine that under such circumstances a regularity in the arrangement will ensue. Suppose that a flat body, shaped like A, had four centres of attraction, two positive and two negative, arranged as shown. If we had to lay a number of such bodies on a flat surface, and so join them together that a positive and a negative centre lay always close to one another, we might arrive at some such arrangement as is shown in Fig. 26.

Whatever arrangement we adopted we should naturally find in the result a certain regularity,

THE NATURE OF CRYSTALS

as in the figure. And apparently Nature works in some such way: the molecules lie side by side in an *ordered array*. The point is of fundamental importance. Order and regularity are the consequence of the complete fulfilment of the attractions which the atoms or molecules exert on one another. When the structure has grown to a size which renders it visible in the microscope, or even to the naked eye, the regularity is manifest in the form of the solid body: it is what we call a crystal. It is bounded by a number of plane faces, often highly polished in appearance, so that the crystal has a certain charm due partly to glitter and sparkle, partly to perfect regularity of outline. We feel that some mystery and beauty must underlie the characteristics that please us, and indeed that is the case. Nature is telling us how she arranges the molecules when given full opportunity. There are but two or three in her unit of pattern, and when the unit is complete it contains every property of the whole crystal, because there is nothing to follow but the repetition of the first design. Through the crystal, therefore, we look down into the first structures of Nature, though our eyes cannot read what is there without the use, so to speak, of strong spectacles, which are the X-ray methods. A few crystal forms are shown in Plate XIII.

There are three stages in the arrangements of matter: the single atom as we find it in helium gas; the molecule as it is studied by the chemist; and the crystal unit which we now examine by X-ray analysis. To take an example, there are the *atoms* of silicon or of oxygen. The *molecule* of silicon dioxide contains one unit of silicon and two units of oxygen, arranged, no doubt, in some special way. Lastly, there is the substance quartz, of which the *crystal unit* consists of three molecules of silicon dioxide, arranged, again, in a special fashion which we now know has a certain screw-like character. The quartz crystal con-

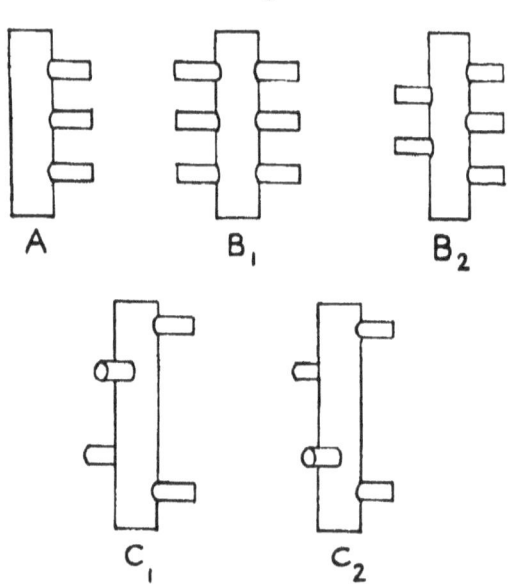

FIG. 27.—Models illustrating screw structure.

A. One sort of peg: *i.e.* every peg is like every other, and all point the same way.

B_1 and B_2. In each of these there are two sorts of peg: *i.e.* one lot of pegs pointing to the right and one to the left. Two varieties of arrangement.

C_1 and C_2. Three sorts of peg: pointing in three different directions. The two arrangements C_1 and C_2 give a right-handed and a left-handed screw respectively.

PLATE XIII

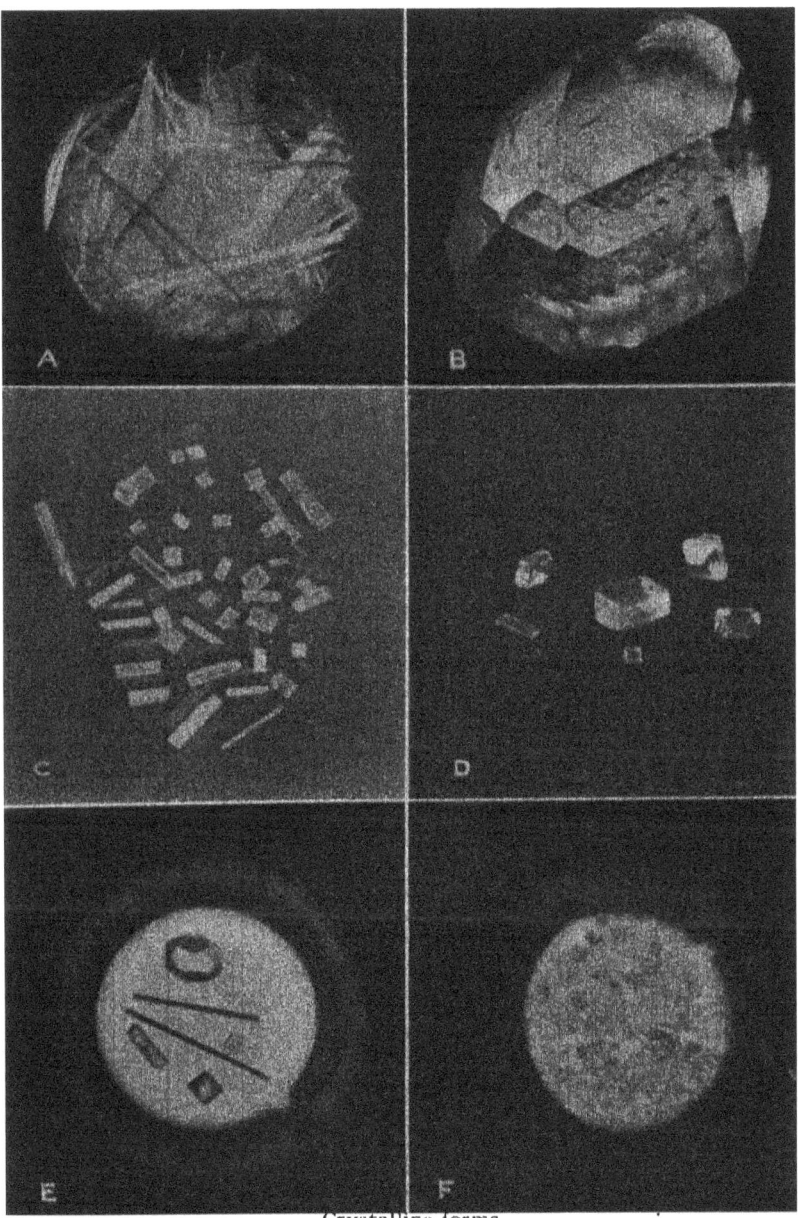

Crystalline forms.

A. Sulphur trioxide crystals which have grown from vapour in a glass vessel. B. Erythritol crystal, grown from solution. C. Ammonium chloride; ideal and distorted cubical crystals from solution containing urea. D. Crystal forms: Quercite; Cocosite. E. Crystal forms: Alizarin, Rubidium alum; Sodium chloride; Ammonium cobalt sulphate; Phthalic acid. F. Ammonium chloride; fern-leaf crystals (octahedral) and cubical crystals from solution containing urea.

THE NATURE OF CRYSTALS

tains an innumerable multiplication of these units. Each of the units has all the properties of quartz, and, in fact, is quartz; but a separate molecule of silicon dioxide is not quartz. For example, one of the best-known properties of quartz is its power of rotating the plane of polarisation of light, and this property is associated with the screw which is to be found in the crystal unit. It takes three molecules to make the screw. If we insert pegs into a round stick as in the figure, and make all the pegs the same in every particular—that is to say, if our unit of pattern contains one peg only—we may form an arrangement like A. With two pegs to the unit of pattern we can make an arrangement like B_1 or B_2. With three pegs to the unit of pattern we may make one as in C, which may twist either of two ways, C_1 or C_2, or, as it is generally said, may be either right-handed or left-handed. The X-rays actually tell us that the quartz unit contains three molecules, and that they are arranged in a screw-like form, with which facts the form of the quartz crystal is in complete agreement, because there are two varieties in the form, as shown in Fig. 27A. In one there is a sequence in the faces x, s, r' which screw off to the right, while in the other they go to the left.

Such a dual arrangement may be expected to be a consequence of the existence of the two kinds of screw, though we do not yet know enough to enable us to guess why these particular faces are prominent. Quartz or "rock crystal" was called "Krystallos" by the Greeks; the name was given to ice also, because the two substances were confused with each other. It is appropriate, therefore, that we should use quartz as an illustration of what is meant by crystal structure and the crystal unit.

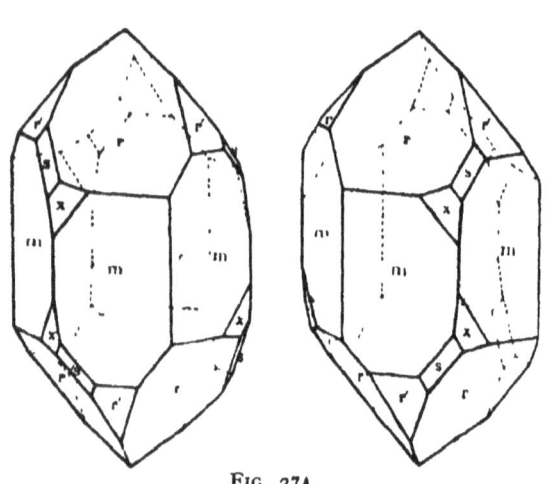

Fig. 27A.

We may now ask ourselves why, if the natural arrangement of molecules is regular, we do not find all bodies in crystalline form. To this we must answer that in the first place a large perfect crystal must grow from a single nucleus. It is difficult to say what first arrests the relative motion of two or three molecules of the cooling liquid, joining them together and making a

THE NATURE OF CRYSTALS

beginning to which other molecules become attached. Perhaps it is a mere accident of their meeting; perhaps some minute particle of foreign matter is present which serves as a base, or some irregularity on the wall of the containing vessel. If there are very many nuclei present in the liquid, very many crystals will grow; and since they are not likely to be orientated to each other when they meet, they will finally form an indefinite mass of small crystals, not a single crystal. They may be so small that to the eye the whole appears as a solid mass without any regularity of form. In order that a large perfect crystal should be formed, the arrangements must be such that the molecules find few centres on which to grow. And they must grow, usually, very slowly and quietly, so that each molecule has time to settle itself correctly in its proper place. The molecules must have enough movement to permit of this adjustment. These conditions are well shown in the methods which the crystallographer employs for the growth of crystals. If, for example, he is growing a large crystal of salt from a solution of brine, he will suspend a minute, well-formed crystal in the brine, and he will keep the temperature of the latter so carefully adjusted that the atoms of sodium and chlorine are only tempted

128   THE NATURE OF THINGS

to give up their freedom when they meet an assemblage of atoms already in perfect array—that is to say, when they come across the suspended crystal. If the solution is too hot, the

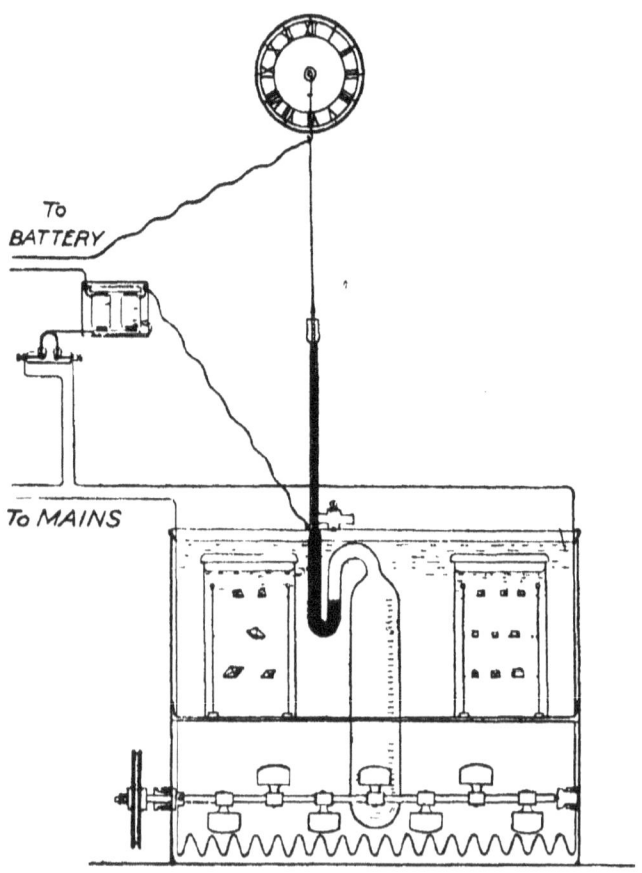

Fig. 28.—The thermostat.

The temperature of the bath in which stand the bottles containing the growing crystals must be free from sudden and irregular variations, and must be slowly lowered day by day. The temperature is maintained by an electric heater; if it rises too high the current is turned off through the expansion of the liquids in the large thermometer which also stands in the bath. The rise of the mercury closes a circuit containing an electromagnet which pulls the switch. The clock is all the time lowering—very slowly—a wire to meet the mercury in the thermometer, so that the temperature at which the heating coil is turned off is being steadily diminished. The heater is at the bottom of the bath, and a stirrer is just above it.

suspended crystal will be dissolved in the unsaturated solution; if it is too cold, crystals will begin to grow at many points. Sometimes the liquid is kept in gentle movement so that various parts of it are brought to the suspended crystal in due turn. The principal conditions are time and quiet, a solution of the salt just ready to precipitate its contents, temperature and strength of solution being properly adjusted for the purpose, the presence of a small perfect crystal and the gentle movement of the solution past it. We do not, of course, quite understand how these or some such conditions come to be realised during the growth of a diamond or a ruby; but we find them to be necessary in the laboratory when we attempt to grow crystals ourselves.

When the conditions are fulfilled in part only, we may get a mass of minute crystals in disarray; we may even find a totally irregular structure—an amorphous substance, to employ the usual phrase. This alone would account for the seeming rarity of crystals, and we have also to bear in mind that many bodies are highly composite in character, consisting of many substances each of which has its own natural form. The X-rays show us that the crystal is not so rare as we have been inclined to think; that even in cases where there is no obvious crystallisation Nature has been attempting to produce regular arrangements, and that we have missed them hitherto because our means of detecting them have been inefficient. The regularity of Nature's arrangement is manifested in the visible crystal, but is also to be discovered elsewhere. It is this regularity which we shall see to be one of the foundation elements of the success of the new methods of analysis.

Let us now turn to the consideration of the X-rays. The reason of their ability to help us at this stage may first be given in general terms.

The X-rays are a form of light, from which they differ in wave length only. The light waves which are sent out by the sun or an electric light or a candle and are perceived by our eyes have a narrow range of magnitude. The length of the longest is about a thirty-thousandth of an inch, and of the shortest about half as much. These sizes are well suited to the purpose for which we employ them. Let us remember that when we see an object we do so by observing the alterations which the object makes in the light coming from the source and reaching our eyes by way of the object. Our eyes and brains have attained by long practice a marvellous skill in detecting and

THE NATURE OF CRYSTALS

interpreting such changes. We may be unsuccessful, however, if the object is too small; and this is not only because a small object necessarily makes a small change in the light. There is a second and more subtle reason : the *nature* of the effect is changed when the dimensions of the object are about the same as the length of the wave, or are still less. Let us imagine ourselves to be walking on the seashore watching the incoming waves. We come in the course of our walk to a place where the strength of the waves is less, and when we look for the reason we observe a reef out to sea which is sheltering the beach. We have a parallel to an optical shadow : the distant storm which has raised the waves may be compared to the sun, the shore on which the waves beat is like the illuminated earth, and the reef is like a cloud which casts a shadow. The optical shadow enables us to detect the presence of the cloud, and the silence on the shore makes us suspect the presence of the reef. Now the dimensions of the reef are probably much greater than the length of the wave. If for the reef were substituted a pole planted in the bottom of the sea and standing out of the surface, the effect would be too small to observe. This is, of course, obvious. Even, however, if a very large number of poles were so planted in the sea so that the effect mounted up and was as great as that of the reef, the resulting shadow would tell us nothing about each individual pole. The diameter of the pole is too small compared with the length of the wave to impress any permanent characteristic on it; the wave sweeps by and closes up again and there is an end of it. If, however, the sea were smooth except for a tiny ripple caused by a breath of wind, each pole could cast a shadow which would persist for at least a short distance to the lee of the pole. The width of the ripple is less than the diameter of the pole, and there is therefore a shadow to each pole.

Just so light waves sweeping over molecules much smaller than themselves receive no impressions which can be carried to the eye and brain so as to be perceived as the separate effects of the molecules. And it is no use trying to overcome our difficulty by any instrumental aids. The microscope increases our power of perceiving small things: with its help we may, perhaps, detect objects thousands of times smaller than we could perceive with the naked eye. But it fails when we try to see things which are of the same size as the wave length of light, and no increase in skill of manufacture will carry us

THE NATURE OF CRYSTALS 133

further. But the X-rays are some ten thousand times finer than ordinary light, and, provided suitable and sensitive substitutes can be found for the eyes, may enable us to go ten thousand times deeper into the minuteness of structure. This brings us comfortably to the region of atoms and molecules, which have dimensions in the various directions of the order of a hundred-millionth of an inch, and this is also the order of the wave lengths of X-rays. Broadly speaking, the discovery of X-rays has increased the keenness of our vision ten thousand times, and we can now "see" the individual atoms and molecules.

We must now connect the X-rays with the crystal, and again we may first state the point in a broad way. Although the single molecule can now affect the X-rays just as in our analogy the single pole can cast a shadow of the fine ripples, yet the single effect is too minute. In the crystal, however, there is an enormous number of molecules in regular array, and it may happen that when a train of X-rays falls upon the crystal the effects on the various molecules are combined and so become sensible. Again, we may make use of an analogy. If a single soldier made some movement with his rifle and bayonet, it might happen that a flash in the sunlight, caused by the motion, was unobserved a mile away on account of its small magnitude. But if the soldier was one of a body of men marching in the same direction in close order, who all did the same thing at the same time, the combined effect might be easily seen. The fineness of X-rays makes it possible for each atom or molecule to have some effect, and the regular arrangement of the crystal adds all the effects together.

We may now consider more in detail the way in which the properties of X-rays and crystals are combined in the new method of analysis. The explanation is, perhaps, a little difficult, and I am trying to state both what precedes and what follows the explanation in such a manner that the explanation can be omitted by those who wish to leave it for a time. It must, however, be mastered sooner or later by everyone who wishes to make use of the new methods.

We have seen that the atoms and molecules of a crystal are in regular array, and have even found reasons for expecting them to be so. Suppose that we stand before the papered wall of a room and consider the pattern upon it. It is a repetition of some unit (Plate XIV B). Mark one particular point of the pattern whenever it

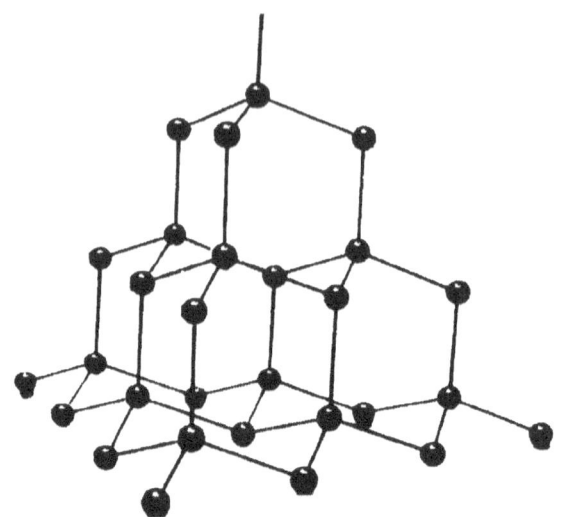

A. Diamond model.

The model shows only the arrangement, and says nothing about the size or shape of the carbon atom.

B. Wall-paper.

The unit cell is outlined in two ways: (a) by thick lines, (b) by thin lines. The

THE NATURE OF CRYSTALS 135

occurs; if a real marking is disallowed, a mental marking must suffice. It will be found that the marks lie on a diamond- or rhombus-shaped lattice, and that this lattice has the same form no matter what point of the pattern has been chosen for the marking. The rhombus will have

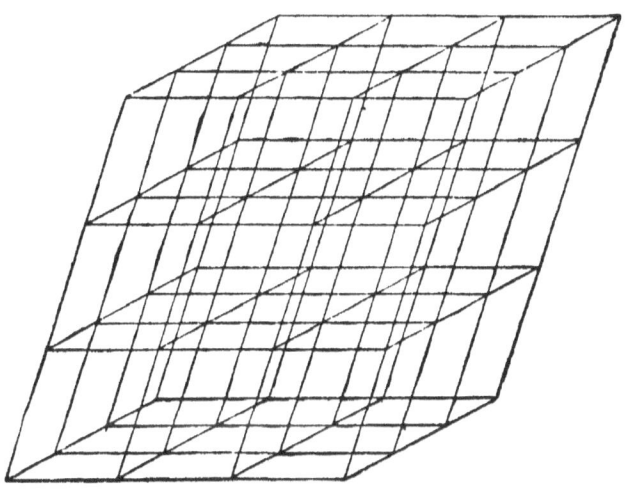

FIG. 29.—Space lattice.

different sizes and shapes in different wall-papers, though the four sides will always be equal or, it may be, the rhombus will be a rectangle, because no one could endure a wall-paper in which this was not the case. The whole pattern of marked points may be called a "lattice." Each rhombus contains the substance of one whole unit of pattern with all its details, and no more.

The arrangement in space of the units of the

crystal is like the arrangement on the wall of the unit of the wall-paper design, except that the plane lattice is replaced by a "space lattice" (Fig. 29). Each little cell of the lattice is bounded by six faces, which are parallel in pairs. The cell can have any lengths of side and any angles; its simplest and most regular form is that of a cube. Each cell contains a full unit of pattern with all its details, and no more: it is the crystal unit, which possesses all the qualities of the crystal, however large the latter may be. In the case of quartz, for example, it has the special shape that is shown in Fig. 30, and it contains three molecules of silicon dioxide. This fact is readily determined by X-ray methods, and also the size and dimensions of the cell, as we shall see; but it is a far more difficult matter to discover the arrangement of the atoms and molecules within the cell.

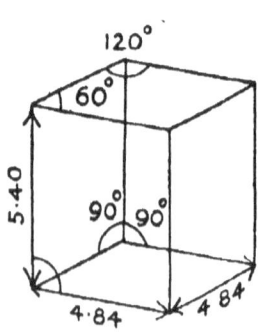

FIG. 30.—Size and dimensions of the unit cell of the quartz crystal in hundred-millionths of a centimetre.

Suppose that we were able to look into a crystal along one of the cell edges of Fig. 29, and found ourselves able to represent what we saw in some such way as is shown in Fig. 31. There is

THE NATURE OF CRYSTALS 137

a grouping of atoms associated with each point on the lattice, which grouping we represent by the entirely imaginary set of circles in the figure. The form of the grouping is of no account, nor its contents; it may contain any number of atoms and molecules, but the essential point is that an exactly similar group is associated with each point on the lattice, as in the design of the wall-paper. Suppose a train of X-ray waves to strike the crystal; in Fig. 32, A, they are

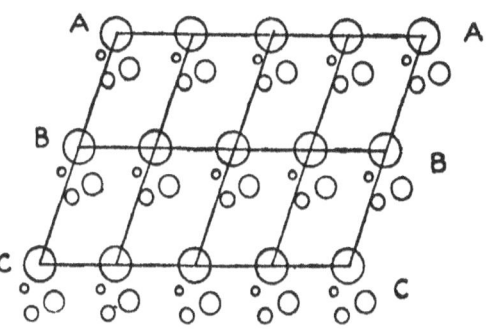

FIG. 31.—An atom group is associated with each point of a lattice.

represented by the line W W and the parallels to W W. When these waves strike the series of groupings strung along AA—each grouping is now represented by a single dot—a new set of similar waves will start from every grouping, though the wave as a whole sweeps on, just as a row of posts planted in the sea would each become the centre of a disturbance when a wave passed by. At a little distance from the row AA these minor disturbances link themselves together in a connected set of waves, represented by the parallel lines *aa*. The effect is analogous to the reflection of sound by a row of palings, or by a stretched piece of muslin. In all cases the bulk of the wave goes on, but there is a reflected wave which makes with the reflecting layer the same angle as the original waves. The reflected waves form a simple train, the same as the original as to wave length, but far weaker, of course: it might be thought that the reflection would simply be a confused mass of ripples, but it is not so. Quite close to the groupings there is some apparent confusion, but a little further along the track of the reflection the wavelets melt into the steadily moving train *aa*, etc.

Behind the row of groupings strung along AA there is another, exactly like the first, which is strung along BB (Fig. 32, B). The original waves, which experiment shows to be very little impaired by their passage over AA, sweep over BB in turn, and again there is a reflection represented by the group of parallel lines *bb*. Behind that there is a row CC forming a *cc* train, a row DD forming a *dd* train, and so on.

As a rule the lines *aa*, *bb*, *cc*, do not coincide with each other. But if the wave length of the rays, the distance between AA and BB (which are really planes seen edgeways), and the angle

THE NATURE OF CRYSTALS

at which the waves meet AA, BB are correctly adjusted to each other, then the lines *aa*, *bb*, etc., do coincide with each other. In actual practice thousands of reflecting planes come into play, and when the reflections all fit together in this way exactly, the whole reflection is strong. If the adjustment is incorrect as it is drawn in the diagram, the reflections do not add together into a sensible effect; some throw their crests, or what corresponds to the crests on a water wave,

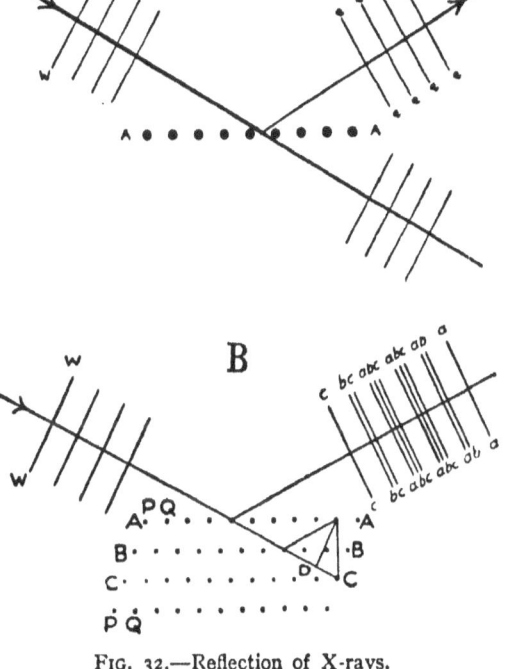

FIG. 32.—Reflection of X-rays.

into the hollows of other waves, and there is mutual interference and annulment. The adjustment has to be exceedingly exact, because there are so many reflecting planes, one behind the other. It is easy to find a formula which expresses the condition for correctness of adjustment, and therefore for reflection. The line A'B'B must be longer than AB by a whole number of wave lengths. If λ is the wave length, d the distance between planes, or spacing, as it is usually called, and θ the angle shown, then:—

$$n\lambda = A'B'B - AB = A'D - AB = DN = 2d\sin\theta,$$

where n is any whole number.

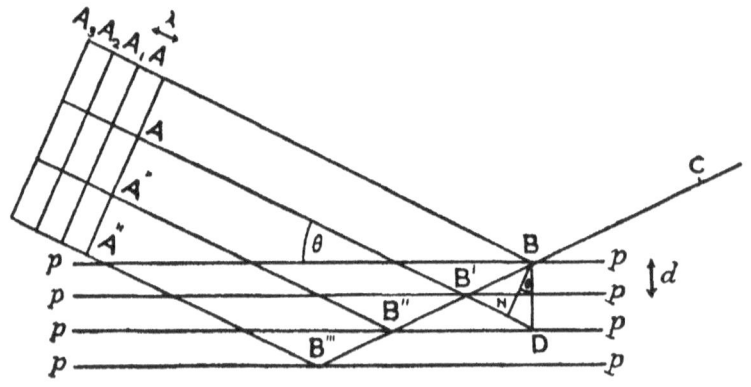

FIG. 33.—The law of reflection of X-rays.

It is not necessary, as I have stated already, for the reader to go through the calculation just given, from which the fundamental equation of the subject is derived.

The essential point is that if the direction of the original rays is gradually altered with respect to the planes AA, BB, etc., there will be *no* observable reflection until the proper inclination is reached; when this happens there is a sudden flash of reflection. The angle of inclination is

THE NATURE OF CRYSTALS

observed; and when, as is always the case in crystal analysis, the wave length of the rays is known, it becomes possible to measure the spacing. The reflected rays cannot, of course, be detected by the eye, but they can make their mark on a photographic plate and be observed in other ways which need not be considered here. The instrument constructed for the purpose of the experiment is called an X-ray spectrometer. It measures the angles at which reflection occurs; and its observations are used to determine spacings in the first instance, and in the second the angles between the various planes of the crystal. For instance, it gives not only the spacings between AA, BB, but also between PP, QQ (see Fig. 32, B), and the angle between AA and PP. It gives, in fact, the dimensions and form of the unit cell.

It is, in general, a simple matter to find by experiment the density of the crystal, and then we can find the weight of the matter contained in the cell. Since we always know the weight of the molecule, it is easy to find how many molecules go to the unit; as already stated, it is always a very small number. Moreover, the observations of the X-ray spectrometer give us some knowledge of the relative positions of the molecules that make up the unit of pattern. They would tell us far more than this if only we knew how to interpret them, but we are too inexperienced as yet. We have found our Rosetta Stone, but are as yet only learners of the new language.

The most important point to bear in mind is that the X-rays give us the distance between any sheet on which the atom groups are spread and the next sheet, which is exactly the same as the first, on which, therefore, another lot of atom groups is spread. This spacing is the same thing as the distance between two opposite faces of the unit cell. We can draw the cell in many ways by joining up different corners of the space lattice. There are not only three spacings to be measured in the crystal, but in reality any number of them; usually we are content to determine a few of them.

In a few cases the crystal analysis has already been carried so far that we know where every atom has its place in the unit of pattern. To get so far we have made use not only of our X-ray analysis, but of many facts of chemistry and physics. I shall not describe these further details, in any case; the general explanation I have given above will serve as a sufficient indication of the methods that have been followed. But I think we shall be interested in some of the results.

THE NATURE OF CRYSTALS 143

First of all let us take the diamond, which is a prince among crystals. It is not only a beautiful and valuable gem, but in its structure it teaches us many things concerning the most fundamental truths of chemistry, particularly organic chemistry. Only one atom, that of carbon, goes to the building of the diamond; but that atom is of vital interest to us. It is a fundamental constituent of foods and fuels, dyes and explosives, of our own bodies and many other things. The structure of the diamond is remarkably simple, though, like all constructions in space, it is difficult to comprehend quickly. We are so accustomed to drawings on the flat, paper and pencil are so handy, that our minds easily grasp the details of a plane design. But we cannot draw in space; we can only construct models at much cost of time and energy, and so our power of conceiving arrangements in space is feeble from want of practice. A few have the natural gift,[1] and some, being crystallographers, have trained themselves to think in three dimensions. Most of us find a great difficulty in our first efforts to realise the arrangements of the atoms and molecules of the crystal. Nevertheless, the diamond structure shown in Plate XIV A will become clear at the cost of a little consideration.

The black balls represent carbon atoms, in respect to position only, not in any way as to size and form, of which we know very little. Every carbon atom is at the centre of gravity of four others; these four lie at the corners of a four-cornered pyramid or tetrahedron, and the first carbon atom is, of course, at the same distance from each of them. We have reason to believe that the ties between the atoms are very strong, and there is only one form of tie throughout the whole structure. In its uniform simplicity and regularity we can surely see the reason why the diamond is placed in the highest class on the scale of hardness. If it is pressed against any other crystal it is the atoms of the latter that must give way, not the atoms of the diamond. The diamond has a cleavage plane. In the figure it is parallel to the plane of the table on which the model stands; there are four such planes, one parallel to each face of the four-faced pyramid. The model can be turned over so as to rest on any one of the four faces, and looks exactly the same in each position. The distance between the centres of two neighbouring carbons is 1·54 Ångström Units; this unit is the hundred-millionth of a centimetre. It does not seem surprising that this particular plane should be

PLATE XV.

[By courtesy of Joseph Asscher & Cie.

A. The Cullinan diamond split into three pieces.
It was originally as large as a small fist.

[By courtesy of Joseph Asscher & Cie.

B. The table and tools used for splitting the diamond.

THE NATURE OF CRYSTALS

the cleavage plane, because it cuts straight across the vertical connections between the horizontal layers that appear in the figure. Each of the layers may be described as a puckered hexagonal network. The crystal may, of course, be considered as an arrangement of layers parallel to any one of the four faces of the tetrahedron, not merely the face on which the model happens to stand.

The existence of this cleavage is well known to diamond cutters, who save themselves much labour by taking advantage of it. In the Tower of London are shown the tools wherewith the great Cullinan diamond was split during its " cutting." Plate XV A shows the diamond in three pieces; and XV B the tools used in splitting it. It is possible to cleave a diamond in yet another plane, which contains any one edge of the tetrahedron and is perpendicular to the other edge; but the operation is difficult and rarely used.

When we consider the diamond construction we cannot but notice the striking appearance, in every part of the model, of an arrangement of the carbon atoms in a ring of hexagonal—or six-sided—form. If we take one of these rings out from the model, it has the appearance of

Plate XVI B, 2: a perfect hexagon when viewed from above, but not a flat ring.

Now the ring of six carbon atoms has already a famous place in chemistry. No one has ever seen the ring: it is too small. But the chemist has inferred its existence by arguments which are most ingenious and most interesting. Even those of us who are not chemists may find no great difficulty in acquiring some understanding of them. For instance, it was well known in the middle of last century that certain molecules could be formed in which the fundamental structure consisted of carbon atoms in a row or chain, and that hydrogen atoms could be attached to the various carbon atoms in such a way that every carbon atom had four other atoms attached to it. That was known because the molecule could not be made to take on any more hydrogens: it was full, or, as the chemists say, "saturated," because a single carbon atom is "saturated" when it has four other atoms attached to it, as, for example, in marsh gas or methane (CH_4). The relative number of carbons and hydrogens was exactly what would be expected on this hypothesis. With six carbon atoms there ought to be fourteen hydrogen atoms, as the diagram shows, and this is found by experiment to be

THE NATURE OF CRYSTALS 147

the case. These substances are called the "paraffins" (see the latter part of the next lecture); the various members of the series having different numbers of carbons in the chain. The particular substance shown in the figure is called hexane.

Now in 1825 Faraday isolated a certain substance from the residue found in gas retorts, which he called bicarburet of hydrogen; it is now known as benzene. A few drops of Faraday's first preparation are preserved as an historical treasure in the Royal Institution. The molecule of this substance contains six carbon atoms like hexane, and six hydrogen atoms. It can be made to take on six more hydrogen atoms, twelve in all, but no more, and the new molecule then behaves chemically like hexane in respect to most of its properties. But it cannot have the same structure as hexane, because it has two hydrogen atoms less. The riddle was solved in 1867 by Kekulé, who suggested that the framework of benzene is a ring, not a chain, of six carbon atoms; we may think of it as derived from the chain of Fig. 34 by the removal of the two hydrogen atoms at the

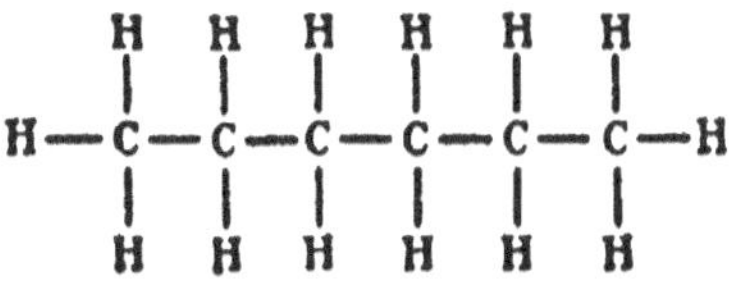

FIG. 34.—Hexane.

ends and a bending of the chain round until the two ends meet and are joined up. We then have the structure shown in Fig. 35. Its chemical name is hexahydrobenzene. Benzene itself has only one hydrogen at each corner of the hexagon. The carbon chain and the carbon ring are the foundations of the two great divisions of organic chemistry. Chain molecules are found not only in the paraffins, but in fats, oils, soaps and many other important groups of substances. The ring is the basis of many thousands of known molecules, including dyes and explosives, drugs such as quinine and saccharin; and so on.

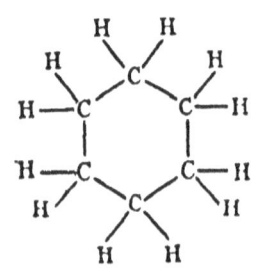

FIG. 35.—Hexahydrobenzene.

The conception of the closed hexagonal ring leads at once to a simple and beautiful explanation of a number of remarkable chemical observations, of which we will consider one example. The benzene molecule consists of the hexagonal ring of carbon atoms, with one hydrogen at each corner. Each carbon atom has only three neighbours in this molecule: it can take on a fourth, so that on the whole there is room for six more atoms or groups of atoms, to be tied on at the corners, and these can be added. But the benzene

THE NATURE OF CRYSTALS 149

molecule can exist contentedly enough without them. Taking the benzene molecule as it is, chemists find that they have the power to alter its constitution, pulling off one or more of the hydrogen atoms, and substituting other atoms or groups of atoms. In a well-known and important case, a single hydrogen is removed and replaced by a group consisting of one carbon and three hydrogen atoms, known as the methyl group. The new molecule has the structure shown in Fig. 36, and is known as toluene, a very important substance, a liquid at ordinary temperatures. A second hydrogen can be removed from the ring molecule and replaced, let us say, by an atom of bromine; the new substance is known as bromotoluene. It is very remarkable that when this has been done three different substances are obtained, all having the same composition, viz. the six carbon atoms, four hydrogen atoms, one bromine atom and one methyl group which we will presume remains intact. How are we to explain the existence of these three, endowed with different properties, yet all having the same constitution? The ring

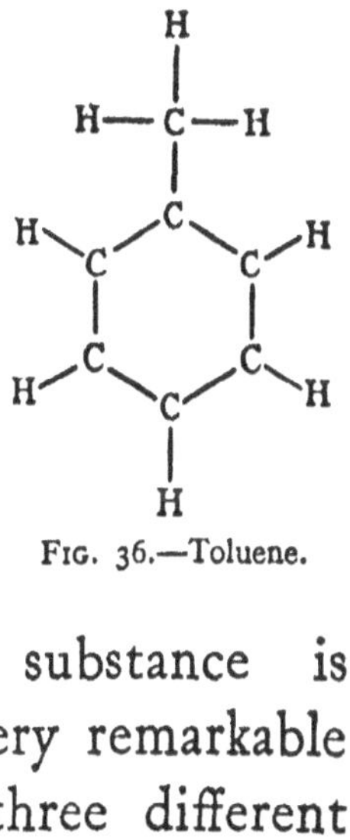

FIG. 36.—Toluene.

hypothesis gives an immediate answer. There are three ways and no more of making the substitutions, which are shown in the figure. The bromine atom may be next to the methyl group, or next but one, or next but two.

The three molecules have different shapes, and therefore may be expected to have different properties; and there is no doubt that there are

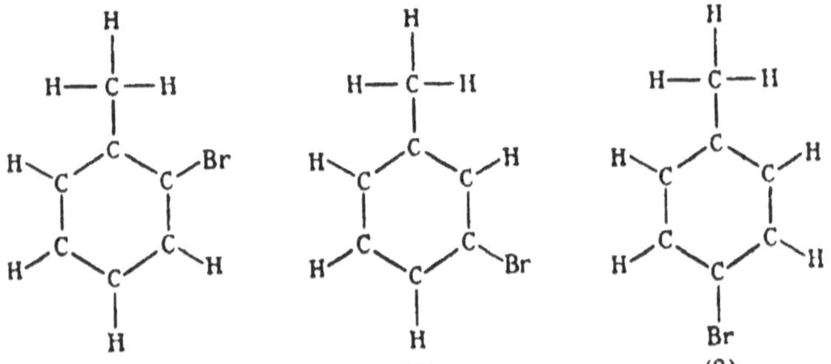

FIG. 37.—Bromotoluene.

actually the three different substances. Chemists have even been able to tell which is which. Many other similar examples could be given, but this one will suffice as an illustration of the significance of position as well as of composition, the three molecules differing only in the relative positions of the two things substituted. The methods of X-ray analysis are peculiarly fitted to deal with such differences as these, because they measure the dimensions of the unit of pattern

THE NATURE OF CRYSTALS

into which two or more molecules are packed, and can detect the effects of altering the *shape* of the molecule. A little work of this kind has already been done.

It is very interesting to observe that in the case of chain molecules the number of carbon atoms is found to vary within wide limits; butyric acid, the substance characteristic of rancid butter, contains four carbon atoms, while palmitic acid, found in palm oil and other places, contains sixteen (see the latter part of the next lecture). On the other hand, the ring molecule of six carbon atoms occurs far more frequently than any other. It must be the easiest to form and the strongest in construction. Now the diamond, the only crystal, except graphite, which consists of carbon atoms only, is full of hexagonal rings. It is natural to suppose that the reason for the ring of six is to be found in the diamond structure. But the basis of the latter is simply the principle according to which each carbon atom is surrounded by four others symmetrically arranged round about it. The two lines which join a carbon atom to two of its neighbours are inclined to one another at an angle readily calculated to be $109° 28'$. If in certain circumstances it is the rule that the junction of two carbon atoms with a third must always be made so as to show this angle, see Fig. 50, then the shortest ring that will close up contains six carbon atoms. (A model may be made to illustrate the point. Wooden balls of sufficiently regular form can be obtained in large numbers, being used in the manufacture of large buttons. Four holes are drilled at the proper places on each ball, and gramophone needles are used as connections. Models of diamond, and many forms of ring and chain molecules can then be put together.) Five carbon atoms in one plane *nearly* make a ring, because the angle of a pentagon is 108°. But if the angle is to be 109° 28′, it is necessary to take six, and to arrange them in the puckered form of Plate XVI B 2. Whether the benzene ring is actually puckered under all circumstances, or is sometimes flat, in which case the angle is 120° (Plate XVI B 1), or even has the shape shown in Plate XVI B 3, which is another form based on the tetrahedral angle, we find it difficult at present to say with any certainty. Experimental evidence is accumulating, but is not yet decisive as to this particular point; perhaps all three forms occur. Meanwhile, many facts emerge in the course of the work which are definite and very interesting.

The remarkable substance graphite is, like

THE NATURE OF CRYSTALS 153

diamond, composed of carbon atoms only. It is much lighter, its density being 2·30 nearly; the density of diamond is 3·52. Clearly, some rearrangement of the atoms has taken place in which the spacings between the atoms have on the average materially increased. The X-rays show that the increase has taken place entirely in one direction. There are layers in graphite as in the diamond structure (Plate XVI A). To one looking down on a layer from above it presents the same appearance of a hexagonal network; and moreover the side of the hexagon is almost exactly the same in length. But the distance between layer and layer has been greatly increased, and it is this change which has made the substance so much lighter. Recent experiments seem to show that the layers have been flattened out, so that each carbon is now surrounded by three atoms in its own plane. If the ties between the atoms in each layer have altered at all, they have at least not lost in strength; on the other hand, the ties between layer and layer are greatly weakened. For these reasons the layers slide over each other very easily, and at the same time each layer is tough in itself. It is the existence of these two conditions that makes graphite so good a lubricant; not only is the readiness to slip of importance, but also the fact that the layer does not easily break up into powder. When one slips on the black-leaded hearthstone, some of the layers are clinging to the stone and some to the sole of one's boot; it is these layers that slide on one another. It is very curious that a single change—whose real nature is, however, a mystery—should convert the substance which is chosen as the type of hardness into one of the most efficient lubricators we possess.

Another set of facts which also supports the idea that the ring is a real thing, having dimensions which can be measured and allowed for, is to be found in the comparison of two crystals, naphthalene and anthracene. These substances are of the greatest importance in the dye industry, the former being used in the manufacture of artificial indigo, the latter in the manufacture of alizarin, which is the active constituent of madder.

Naphthalene is a common substance; to most of us it is no doubt familiar in the form of the white, strongly smelling balls which we put into drawers to keep the moth away. If naphthalene is dissolved in ether, and the solution allowed to dry off gradually, the crystals are readily formed.

THE NATURE OF CRYSTALS

In general appearance they resemble the crystals illustrated in Plate XIII D.

The chemist finds that naphthalene consists of a double benzene ring which we draw as in Fig. 38, A; anthracene is based on a treble ring, Fig. 38, B. When crystals of the two substances are subjected to X-ray analysis, it is found that the unit of pattern contains two molecules and that the shape of the cell which contains the unit is as shown in Fig. 39. The dimensions of the cells are given below the figures. If the two cells are compared with each other, it is noteworthy that along two of the edges the cells are very nearly the same size; but that there is a great difference in respect to the third. The natural inference is that the double and treble ring molecules lie parallel to OC in the two cases, and that the difference between 11·18 and

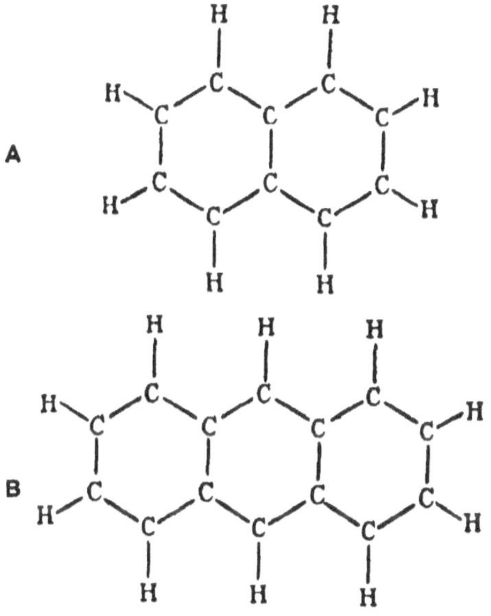

FIG. 38.—Naphthalene and anthracene.

8·69 is to be ascribed to the extra length of the molecule. The anthracene contains one more ring than diamond, which gives it the extra length, 2·49. Now if we measure the width of the ring as it occurs in diamond, it is found to be 2·50. Thus we again find support for the view that the ring has a definite form, and nearly

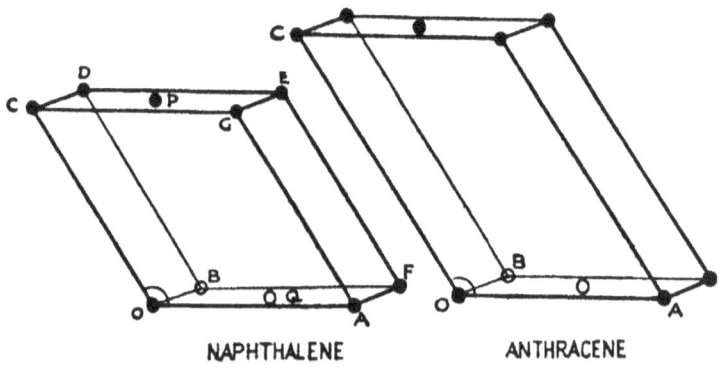

FIG. 39.—Unit cells of naphthalene and anthracene, drawn to the same scale.

	OA	OB	OC	
Naphthalene.	8·34	6·05	8·69	Figures in Ångström
Anthracene.	8·58	6·02	11·18	Units: see p. 144.

constant dimensions; so that we have something to guide us in trying to discover the structure of a crystal of which the ring forms part. The X-rays tell us the size and form of the unit cell, and how many molecules it contains, as well as certain information about the relative positions of the molecules. If we know the size, more or less accurately, of the ring or rings which form

THE NATURE OF CRYSTALS 157

part of the molecule, we can set out on the investigation of the structure, knowing that bodies of definite dimensions have to be fitted into cells of definite shape. Work of this kind is extraordinarily interesting, since it gives us new knowledge of the arrangements of the atoms in the organic molecules and of the forces that bind the atoms in the molecule and the molecule in the crystal. It is a new field of inquiry, in which some results are definite and clear, others more obscure and difficult to interpret until greater experience has been obtained.

The organic molecule appears to us so far as a light rigid framework, in itself tightly held together, but weakly joined to its neighbours in the crystal. Organic substances are nearly always light, not very much heavier than water. The fact that the density of naphthalene is only 1·15 shows the emptiness of its structure. Even the diamond is full of holes, like a sponge. If the holes were filled up by other carbon atoms, the density of the diamond would be doubled, for each hole is just large enough to take one more carbon atom, and there are as many holes as there are atoms.

The weakness of the bonds that join molecule to molecule is the cause of the softness of the organic crystal and of the ease with which it can be melted. For the same reason naphthalene "sublimes": it evaporates while in the solid state. Whole molecules are flung off from the solid, and form a vapour which may crystallise again in a cooler part of the containing vessel.

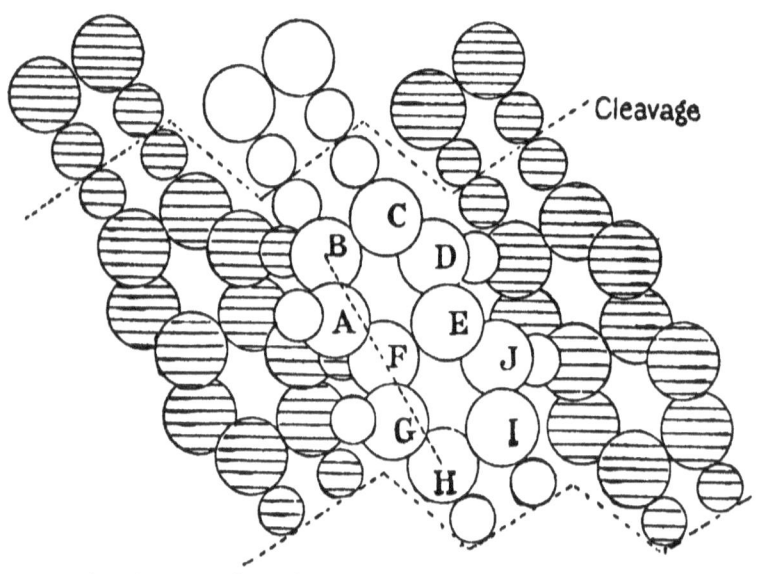

FIG. 40.—Showing mutual relations of three naphthalene molecules and parts o others.

Naphthalene and anthracene are flaky in structure: they have, as it is said, a well-developed cleavage. The dotted lines show the cleavage plane; clearly the molecules break away from each other more easily at the ends than at the sides. In each flake the molecules stand nearly upright, like corn leaning over in the wind.

THE NATURE OF CRYSTALS

The general conclusion to which we are led by these considerations is that the "benzene ring" is a real material object of definite form and dimension, which is built into crystalline structures with little alteration of form. We must now go on to consider the "chain" molecule: the basis of as great a section of organic chemistry as that which rests on the ring. As this lecture is already long enough, we can consider the chain in our next lecture, in addition to the ice crystal, which will be our main subject.

LECTURE V

THE NATURE OF CRYSTALS: ICE AND SNOW

WHEN we look round to see what crystals we shall examine by our new X-ray analysis, the crystals of ice and snow at once strike our imagination. Water is one of the most obvious substances in the world: it affects our lives in numberless ways and we are interested in all the forms which it can assume. And again, from a scientific point of view we should like to discover the structure built with so simple a molecule, one oxygen and two hydrogens, and we might find that it was within our power to do so. But there is one very compelling reason in the beauty of the snow crystal, with its tracery so delicate and finished, and of the frost crystals on the window-pane, so quaint and charming in their outline. It is true that the blocks of ice that come from the freezing works are not remarkable for grace of outline, though there is a fascination in watching them slither across the pavement at the end of the ice-man's pincers.

PLATE XVII.

A

B
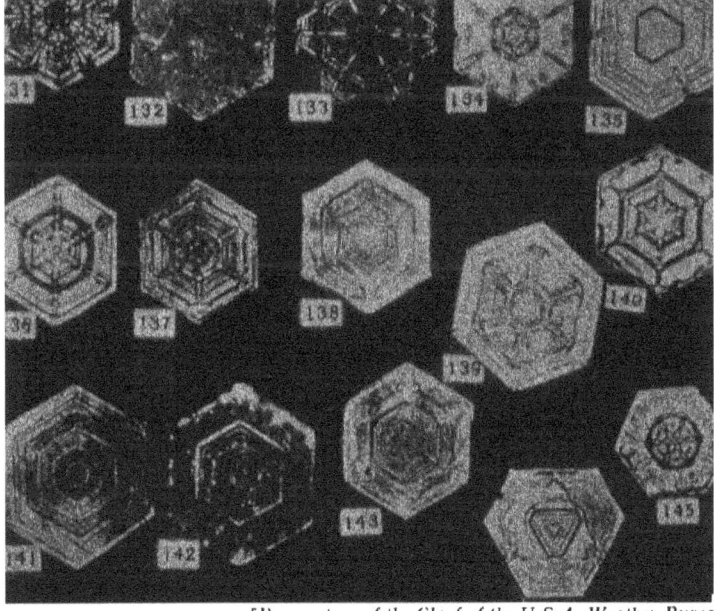

[By courtesy of the Chief of the U.S.A. Weather Bureau.
Snow crystals of various forms.
(From *Monthly Weather Review*, U.S.A.)

PLATE XVIII.

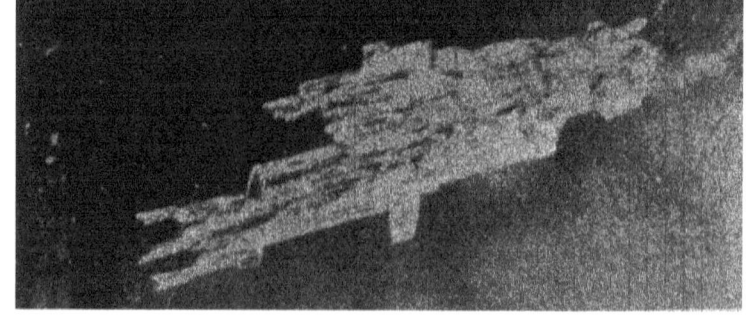

[*By courtesy of the Dept. of Scientific Research of the Admiralty*
A. Snow crystals. (From the Monthly Weather Bureau, U.S.A.)
B. Ice flowers growing on the ice floes. C. Bundle of irregular prisms.
(From "The British Antarctic Expedition, 1910-1913.")

THE NATURE OF CRYSTALS

The manufacture of commercial ice is too rapid to bring out the ice design: the crystalline structure is there, but the mass contains a multitude of tiny invisible crystals oriented in all directions, and is full of bubbles and sheets of air.

If we are to see what Nature will do if left to work out her design in peace, we must examine the snowflakes that fall in a hard northern winter. In England, we do not see the best crystals: it is not cold enough. Observers in other countries such as Sweden and America have many exquisite drawings, which are to be found scattered through physical and meteorological publications. Some of them are reproduced in Plates XVII and XVIII.

We can imagine the way in which the snowflakes grow. One or two molecules of water become associated in the upper air; molecule after molecule adds itself to the growing, falling crystal, filling out the details of the pattern until at last the six-pointed snowflake rests gently on the ground. If the weather is cold the flake may continue to grow in the same way, and the crystals develop perfect little facets, which glitter like diamonds in the sunshine. When the snow crystal first forms, it is very often feathery; the six arms grow outwards and other little arms grow out from each of them to right and left, and from these yet smaller arms, and so on; all the arms joining each other at the angle of 60°, so that the whole is like a six-pointed star of fine lace. These feathery forms are peculiar to the early stage of crystallisation, and seem to be the consequence of sudden and rapid freezing. The arms stretch out from the centre because they have used up the nearer molecules that are ready to join up into the structure, and they must stretch out into new fields. This effect is often found in other cases of rapid crystallisation; a notable example is the formation of skeleton crystals of iron in the crucible of molten and cooling metal. If they are to be preserved, the rest of the liquid must be poured off before the crystal has had time to fill up vacant spaces. They are called "dendrites," because they look something like trees, with trunks, big branches, small branches, and so on, but the angle at which two branches of an iron crystal join together is a right angle, not 60°, and the form is far from being as graceful as that of ice.

When the snow crystal has had time to grow, and there is an available supply of molecules, the gaps fill up, and the crystal becomes a hexagonal plate (Plate XVII B). Sometimes, it is supposed,

PLATE XIX.

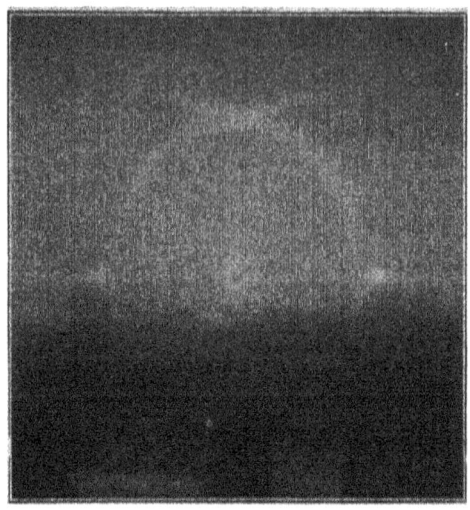

The first picture is due to Mr G. A. Clarke, and is taken from Mr. F. J. Whipple's article on Meteorological Optics in the "Dictionary of Applied Physics," Vol III, p. 529 (by courtesy of Messrs Macmillan & Co). It shows a halo and mock suns. The second picture is from an interesting original sketch in the possession of the Royal Institution. It shows the halo and the "sun-pillar."

THE NATURE OF CRYSTALS

the plates grow in that form from the beginning. Strange to say, these plates are often connected in pairs by a hexagonal prism; one plate is generally larger than the other, and the whole is like a fairy tea-table (Plate XVIII A). The prism appears also in the curious formations of Plate XVIII C, which is taken from Wright and Priestley's "Glaciology," British Antarctic Expedition, 1910-1913.

The prisms and plates and "tea-tables" are believed to be the cause of the mock suns and halos

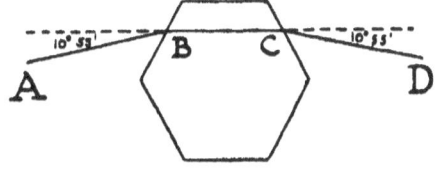

FIG. 41.
The hexagon represents a magnified section of an ice prism. ABCD is a ray passing through it.

that are observed in high latitudes (Plate XIX).

Suppose that the hexagon in Fig. 41 represents a section of one of these prisms or plates, and let ABCD be the path of a ray of light going through it. It is refracted at the points B and C; the ray is on the whole bent through an angle of at least 21° 50′, which is, in the language of physics, the angle of minimum deviation. If in Fig. 42 S be a source of light and E the eye, a ray from S is bent in going through P, and will enter the eye if P is properly placed. In the figure the prism is placed symmetrically, in which case it is known that the deviation SPE has its minimum value. Any prism lying between SPE and SP'E, such as P_0, will bend the ray from S in such a direction that it cannot possibly get to the eye, no matter how the prism is placed. The eye cannot receive a refracted ray from any such prism. A prism P_1 may send light to the eye,

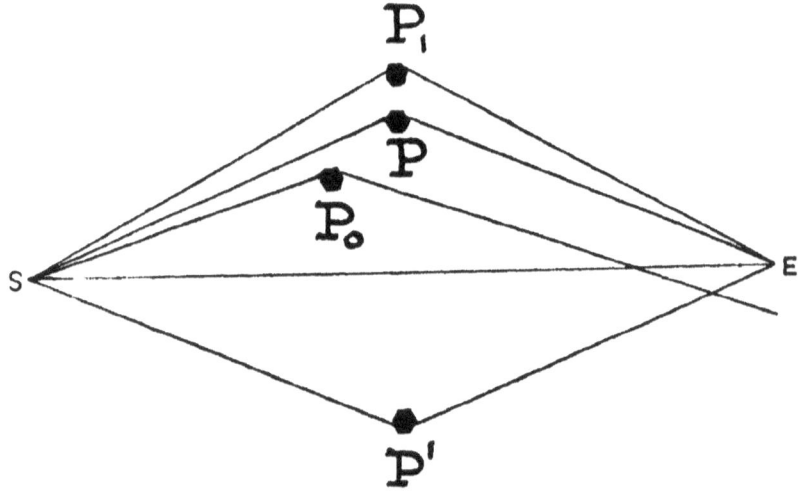

FIG. 42.—Shows how the ice halo is formed. For a description see the text.

if it has an unsymmetrical position, as the figure shows; the angle of deviation has to be more than the minimum, and that is why the prism must be crookedly placed, as in the figure. If, therefore, an observer at E stands facing the sun at S, light will be seen to come from the directions PE and P'E, and also other directions outside; but the latter will be relatively feeble, because most of the deviations are not far from the

THE NATURE OF CRYSTALS 165

minimum value—the further they are from it, the fewer they are, in accordance with a known law of maximum or minimum values. Also there is no light at all from within PEP', and the consequence is that the strong light of the minimum deviations is the more sharply defined.

This applies to rays coming from all directions round the sun; and so, on the whole, the observer must see a ring round the sun, sharp on the inside, rather more diffuse on the outer. For red light the angle PEP' is rather smaller than for blue, so that the halo is not quite white, but is coloured, red on the inside, blue on the outside. The halo is observed if there are enough ice prisms in the air, just as a rainbow is seen if there is a sufficiently large number of drops of rain. When a ray of light goes into a raindrop and out again it is bent through an angle of more than two right angles, so that to see a rainbow one must have the sun at one's back.

A little model may help to make this explanation clearer. The arc-lamp at S in the figure is the source, the eye is at E. Between S and E is a stand on which an arm is mounted; the latter carries a glass prism. The dimensions of the model are so adjusted that a ray of light refracted by the prism falls on E. If the arm swings

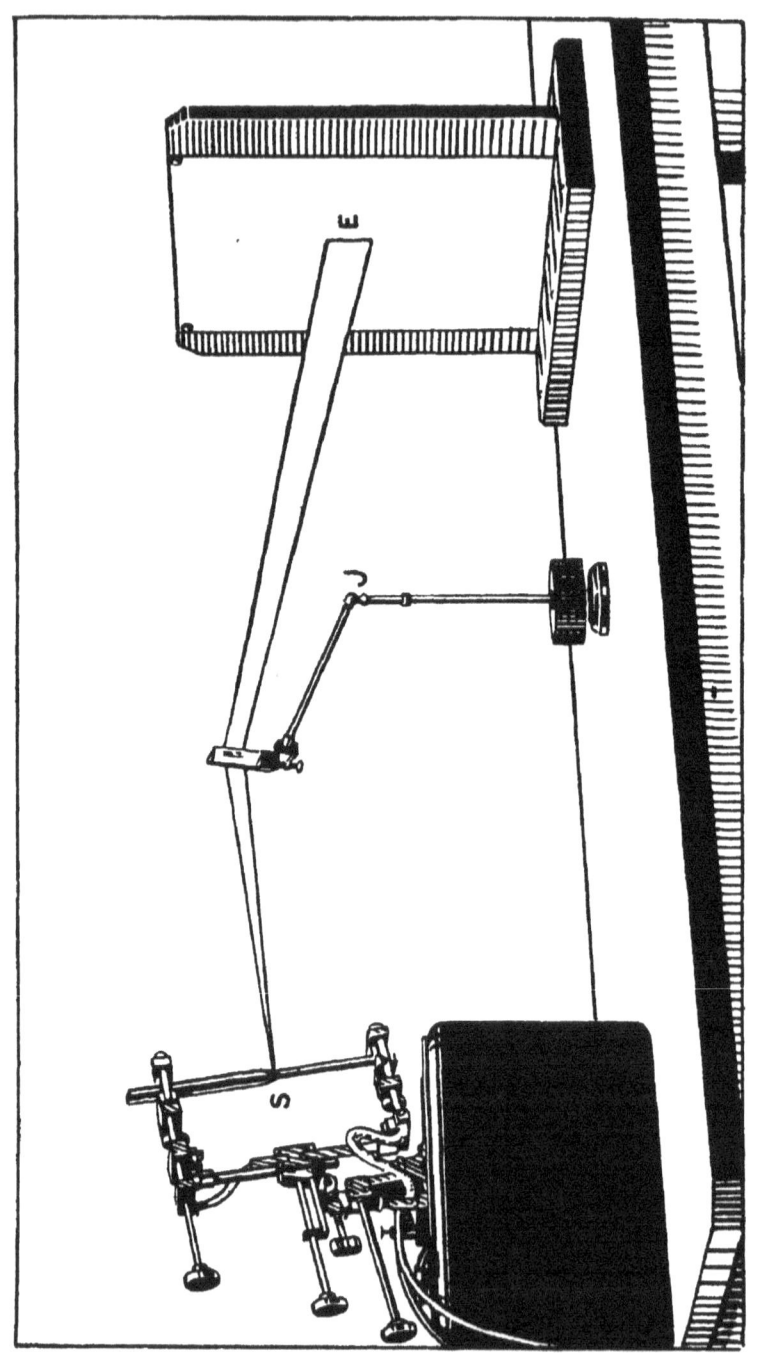

FIG. 43.—Model showing the formation of the ice halo. SJE should be in the same line. For a description see the text.

THE NATURE OF CRYSTALS

round J, the eye continues to be illuminated. If there were prisms all round the circle, the eye would see a circle of light round the central spot.

If for any reason the prisms tended to set themselves in certain positions only, the halo would be incomplete. Something of this kind actually happens. When a long prism falls through the air, the axis tends to set itself horizontally. If, however, it has the tables at the ends, as shown in Plate XVIII A, or if it is simply a hexagonal table which may be considered as a very short prism, its axis tends to become vertical, or, in other words, the table itself to become horizontal. This rather strange effect is in accordance with a well-known rule concerning the movement of bodies through gases or liquids. They tend to set themselves so as to offer as much opposition to the motion as possible. If we make a packet of two or three letters or postcards, and drop them from a height, holding them horizontally and taking the hand quickly from underneath, they remain level throughout the fall. But if we let them fall edge first, they subsequently turn over and over. When we drop a white plate into the water, we see it swaying from side to side, but always tending to the horizontal position. The consequence is that the falling shower of ice crystals contains an undue proportion of vertical and horizontal crystals. Those parts of the halo which lie at the ends of the horizontal and vertical diameters are emphasised, and are like bright spots on the ring: they are often spoken of as mock suns.

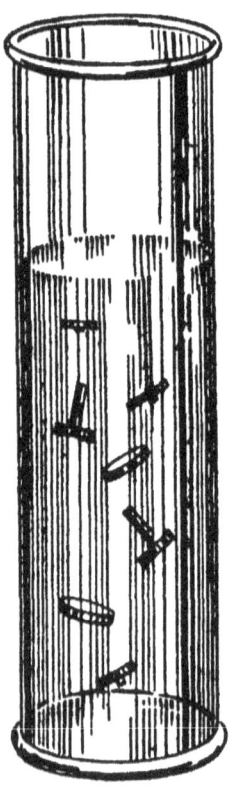

Fig. 44.—Flat discs, and prisms some of which end in discs, falling through water in a tall jar.

It is easy to show the tendency of the "tea-table" forms to become vertical as they fall. We make a number of models of ebonite and allow them to fall in a tall jar full of water. A very tall jar is the best, but even if the depth is not more than eighteen inches or so the tendency is quite obvious. Curiously enough, some of the bodies tend to fall with the plate leading the way, and some with the plate in the rear. The point was examined mathematically by Besson, who showed that when the diameter of the plate is small compared to the length of the prism, the plate tends to go first, and vice versa. We can prove this by experiment; it is best to hold the

THE NATURE OF CRYSTALS 169

axis horizontally under the surface of the water and then let go.

The whole of the vertical line through the centre of the halo is often illuminated also, but this is due to a different reason altogether: it is caused by reflection at the flat surfaces of the snow crystals and plates. Consequently the observer receives reflections of the sun from snowflakes at all altitudes, but they must all lie in a vertical plane through the sun. The bright vertical line is called a "sun-pillar."

Ice when it forms quietly on a water surface exposed to the sky crystallises in a form analogous to that of the snow crystal, all the six-sided figures being horizontal. That it does so is not generally very obvious, though in books of Arctic exploration pictures are to be found of table ice breaking up into six-sided vertical columns, like the basalt columns of the Giants' Causeway. It is also said that when the ice on a lake breaks up, it first divides into vertical columns, which for a time hold each other up; when, however, the ice begins to move, the collapse is rapid and the lake clears quickly.

In the accounts given by Antarctic explorers, it is especially mentioned that the ice on fresh-water lakes was found to be divided into six-sided prisms, all standing upright on the surface. The planes of separation were marked by lines of air bubbles. On the sea ice the formation of the crystals led to an expulsion of the salt which was deposited in the spaces between the crystals, and sometimes squeezed out above the top surface. The prisms were nearly free from salt inside, and fairly fresh water could be obtained if the outside

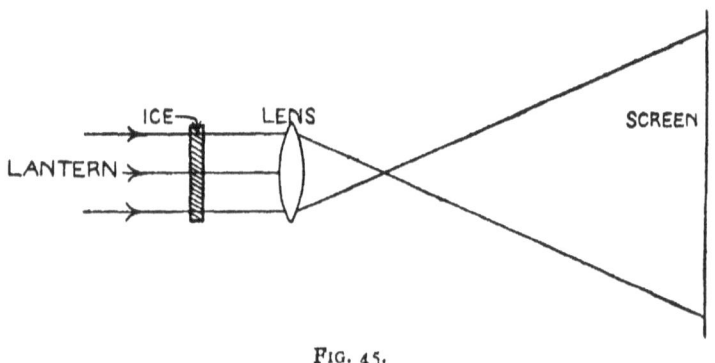

FIG. 45.

layers were first melted off. They were clear crystals, through which an observer might look at the rocks underneath as through tubes.

There is a very beautiful way of observing the crystalline structure of ice, which is described by Tyndall in his book on "Heat."

A slab of clear ice is placed in the rays from an arc lamp and is focused on the screen, as in Fig. 45. The heat of the lantern begins to "undo" the crystals, which come to pieces in

THE NATURE OF CRYSTALS 171

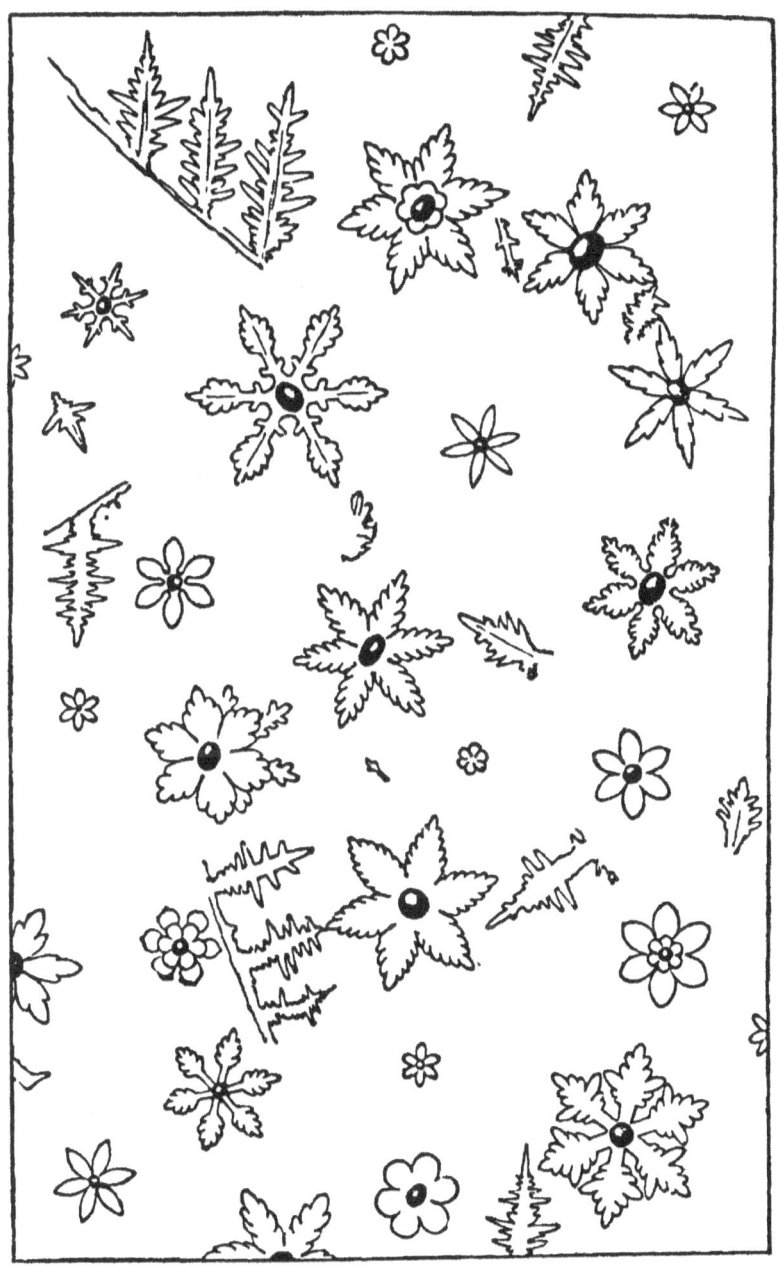

FIG. 45A.—This illustration of the "flowers of ice" is taken from the original sketch in Tyndall's "Heat." It represents a certain stage in the growth of the flowers: at a later stage the whole screen is covered with interlacing figures.

the order inverse to that in which they were put together. Little six-rayed cavities appear and grow, looking like flowers of six petals, and other cavities having a fern-like form in which the fronds are inclined to the stem at an angle of 60°. Soon the whole screen is covered with these "flowers of ice," as they are called: it looks like a beautiful carving in low relief. The ordinary commercial ice does not show the effect; there is a specially prepared "plate ice" which is fairly satisfactory. But the natural ice that is formed in the open at night-time is far better than anything frozen under the usual conditions of ice manufacture. Many disappointing trials were made to prepare a satisfactory experiment for these Christmas Lectures. After all, there was a kindly frost on the night before, and a young enthusiast rode out on his bicycle and collected from a pond a number of pieces which showed the effect splendidly. It is clearly essential that the ice should grow quietly; probably it is also a condition that the water should lose heat quietly at one face, as the water of a pond does on a still, frosty night.

A little black spot often appears in the centre of the ice flower. Tyndall was greatly interested in it, and explained its occurrence. When the

THE NATURE OF CRYSTALS

ice melts within the block and a cavity is formed, the water due to the melting occupies less volume than the ice from which it came. Perhaps it holds together at first in a highly strained condition and fills as water the space it filled as ice. But if so the strain must be very great; it breaks away from the ice and shrinks to its natural volume. A vacuum is left, which acts as a tiny lens and diffuses the light that crosses it. Hence the black spot, which implies the absence of light going straight through the cavity.

The ice flowers can be seen in glacier ice, where they are produced by the heat of the sun. When a glacier is formed by the contributions of ice from tributary glaciers or from blocks that have fallen in on the sides, the mass may consist of a pile of ice masses all frozen together, each of them showing ice flowers. The orientation of the flowers shows in each case the original lie of the block, for they are always formed in planes which were once horizontal. In the figure (Plate XX A), taken from an old volume by Agassiz, a section of glacier ice shows well the various positions of the cavities—some in full view, some on edge, and some in intermediate positions.

Let us now turn to the analysis of the structure of the ice crystal which X-rays have made possible.

We must hope to find in it some explanation for its form and other physical properties which we have been considering. It turns out that the structure is something like that of diamond: there is the same symmetrical arrangement of four neighbours of like kind round every atom. In this case, it is the oxygen atom that stands at the centre of a tetrahedron, four other oxygen atoms lying at the four corners. There are, however, certain minor differences of structure. In the first place, in diamond the carbon atoms join on to each other. In ice there are the hydrogens to be placed. If we put one hydrogen between each pair of oxygens we shall have a symmetrical arrangement in which the atoms are in the proper numerical proportion. Every oxygen has four hydrogen neighbours, and every hydrogen has two oxygen neighbours, which implies that there are twice as many hydrogens as oxygens. A model showing the arrangement under these conditions is illustrated in Plate XX B, C. The large balls represent oxygen, the small represent hydrogen. It must be clearly understood that the X-ray methods do not measure the size of the oxygen atom, or of the hydrogen. All that they do is to find the distance between the centre of one oxygen and the centre of an oxygen neighbour, a distance which

PLATE XX.

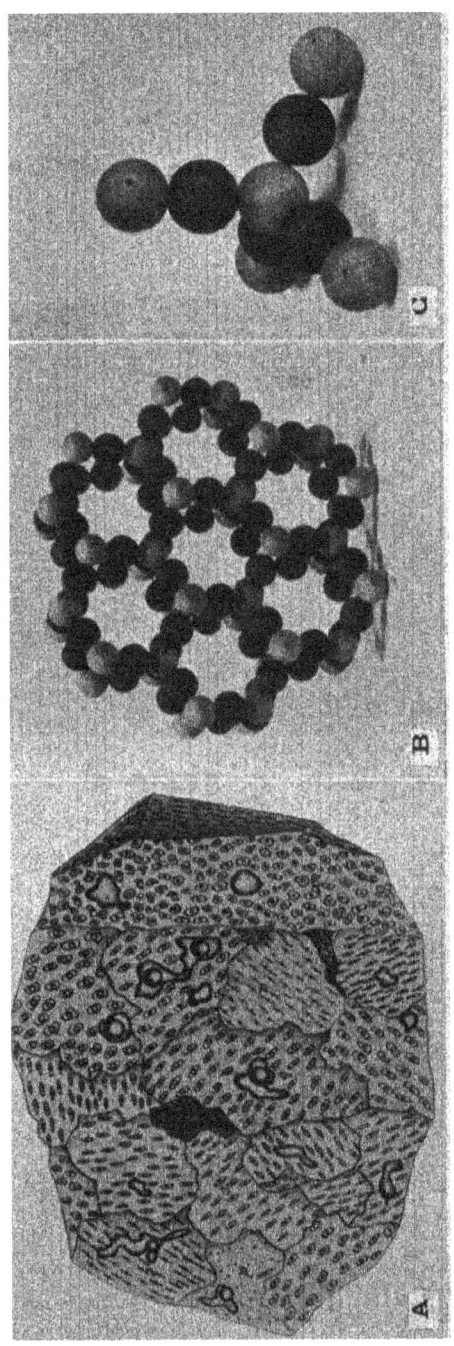

A. This is due to Agassiz. It shows that the mass of glacier ice is an agglomeration of smaller blocks in which, when first laid down, the ice flowers would be in a horizontal plane The blocks have now been heaved into various positions, and the flowers are seen some edgeways, some in full face, and in various other positions. B. The model is made of balls of two colours, the white representing oxygens and the black hydrogens.
C. A smaller section of the ice model, showing the grouping of the oxygens and hydrogens.

THE NATURE OF CRYSTALS 175

is the sum of the diameters of oxygen and hydrogen. The oxygen atom may take all the room, and the hydrogen none, because the hydrogen atom is supposed to hand over its electrons to the oxygen and be left a bare nucleus. No one can say how its size should then be represented. In making a model we must adopt some sizes for the balls which represent the atoms, and the model must be interpreted with the corresponding reservation.

There is a second point of difference between diamond and ice which is subtler and more difficult to realise; but it is worth while trying to understand it. If the reader finds it too difficult to grasp, he may leave it out without any fear of losing the thread of the story.

Suppose that we are looking down on the diamond model from above, and we see a single puckered layer, as in Fig. 46, A. The carbon atoms are marked as 1, if they lie directly on the base of the crystal, and as 1′ if they are the atoms which are somewhat raised above their neighbours in the layer. Take another layer exactly like the first, and write 2 everywhere instead of 1, and place it on the first, so that each 2 comes over a 1′—that is to say, an atom in the lower level of the second layer comes over an atom in the higher level of the first. This is what happens in diamond. The combination is shown in Fig. 46, B, where 1'2 means that the atom 2 lies over the atom 1'. Now take a third layer, which

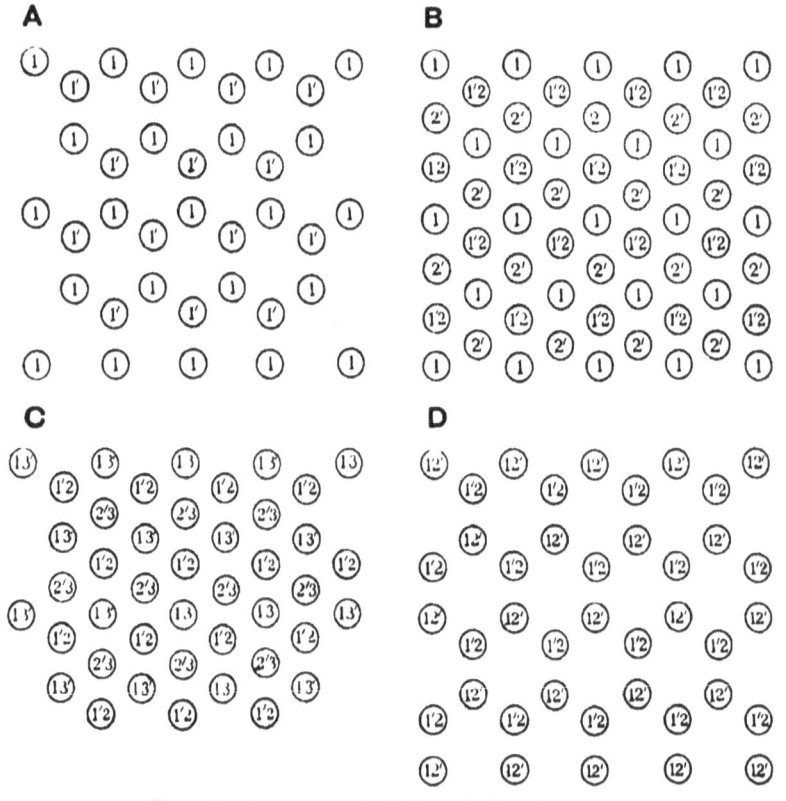

FIG. 46.—Arrangement of atoms in ice structure.

we may denote by using 3's, and lay this so that 3 comes over 2'. We then get the arrangement of Fig. 46, C, and when this is repeated over and over again, in the same order 1 2 3 1 2 3, we get the diamond structure.

THE NATURE OF CRYSTALS

If now we begin again with a layer of 1's, but take as the arrangement of a layer of 2's that which is shown in Fig. 46, D—which, it must be carefully observed, is not the same as before; the layer of 2's has been turned round in its own plane through 180°—we then repeat the first layer, and alternately have 1 and 2. This gives us the arrangement of the oxygens in ice. The structure is complete when we place a hydrogen between each pair of oxygens.

If we look at the picture of the ice model shown in Plate XX B, we may be able to realise the arrangement. Why one crystal should repeat continually a series of three layers, and the other of only two, we cannot imagine.

If we now look at the model of the ice structure we can see in it many interesting features which help to explain what we know of the properties of ice. The hexagonal structure is there, of course, and the emptiness of the model is surely connected with the lightness of ice and the featheriness of snow. Ice floats on water; we can see that the molecules of water when they join up in the crystal structure must take up more room than before. We could obviously crush the model together into a smaller space, and that is, no doubt, what happens when ice melts under pressure. There is a well-known experiment which illustrates the point. A block of ice is supported at its ends, and a fine wire carrying heavy weights is slung over it, as shown in Fig. 47. The wire proceeds to sink slowly into the ice, but as it does so the ice closes up behind it, and when, finally, the

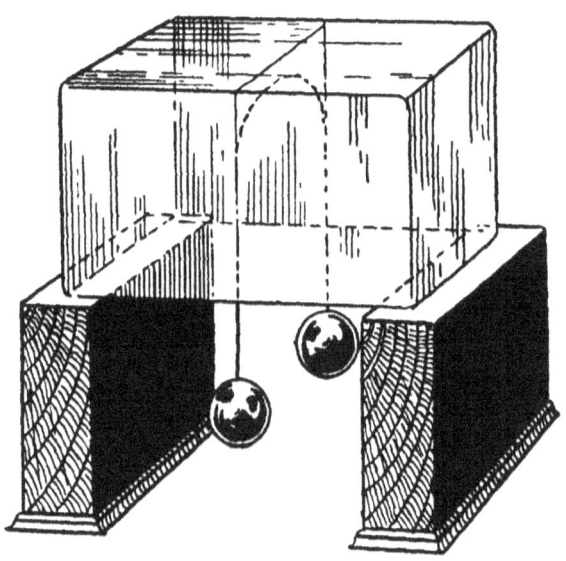

FIG. 47.—Wire cutting through ice (from Tyndall).

wire makes its way right through the block and drops, with the weights, on the floor, the block is still whole. It would seem that the pressure of the wire on the block breaks down the structure of the ice, and some of the molecules are set free. In other words, a certain quantity of ice is melted under pressure and becomes water, which is squeezed out from under the wire and slips round

THE NATURE OF CRYSTALS 179

to the vacant space above it. There it joins up again with the ice on either side. We can imagine the molecules as settling into their places, because on either side there is crystalline ice holding out hands to them.

Crushed ice can be moulded under great pressure into various shapes. We may, for instance, make a crystal cup: we need two or

FIG 48.—Ice moulds and the making of a cup (from Tyndall).

three boxwood moulds of the proper shape. In one we can form the upper portion of the cup in another the stem, and in yet another the foot; then we join them together into one piece by holding them into position for a few moments. The moulds we use in making the cup shown in Fig. 48 were once used by Tyndall for the same purpose.

When Tyndall showed these experiments he was proposing a theory of the movement of glaciers, and employed them as an illustration of his arguments. Tyndall, we may remember, devoted a great deal of time to the measurement of glacier movements: he was interested in them both from the scientific point of view and from his devotion to mountaineering.

Glaciers descend from the snow-covered mountains, glide along the valleys, and pour out into the plains almost as if they were fluid: a very viscous, treacly fluid, because the motion is so slow—a few inches a day or even less in some cases, many feet a day in others. That which has always excited wonder and interest is the stateliness of the motion, and the strange way in which a substance so brittle and crystalline can flow like a river, can move round the corners of a valley, or fall over a cliff and yet remain whole. In Tyndall's time much consideration was given to a theory which supposed that the glacier melted internally in places where the strain was great, and that the water thus formed slipped away, relieving the pressure. It would freeze again, it was said, if it made its way into empty cracks or spaces where there was no longer the pressure required to keep it molten. Thus the glacier would, in a way, contract where compressed and expand elsewhere, and so accommodate itself to

THE NATURE OF CRYSTALS 181

its bed. The explanation seems to offer difficulties when we think of the glaciers in the Arctic or Antarctic which also flow, though the temperature is so low that no conceivable pressure would bring about any melting.

It is possible that when we look a little more closely into the behaviour of a crystalline structure we shall find another way of conceiving how the motion takes place : not so very different in reality from the view that Tyndall maintained, but not so open to criticism. There are many substances that can be made to flow like a glacier : metals can be squirted through holes; wires can be drawn; plates can be rolled. Even the surface of glass, or of a perfect crystal such as Iceland spar, can be made to " flow," as Sir George Beilby has shown. Now all these things are crystalline; if we did not know it before, the X-rays have emphasised the fact for us. And they are just as crystalline after the flow as before. We shall see some examples when we come to speak of the metals. The substance accommodates itself to pressure, changing its shape as it does so. Whole layers of atoms or molecules are momentarily uprooted from their places, ride over the tops—so to speak—of the atoms on which they lie, and settle down into a new position, or perhaps are kept on the move for some time. When they settle down again for a moment the crystal is perfect once more, and when they are uprooted, the bonds are broken as if the substance was going to melt. This must be especially the case when, as in ice, the substance contracts on melting, when the bonds, breaking under pressure, let the atoms and molecules take up positions in which less space is occupied than before. When a piece of metal is bent or squeezed into a new form, the crystals of which it is made, whether few or many, are "sheared"—that is to say, one part slides on another part; and we can understand how many successive "shears" can bring about any change of shape. So it may be in the case of ice: both shearing and melting may be called into play during the change of shape. The "shearing" of ice has often been observed. A block of ice is cut from the ice that has formed naturally on the surface of the water. If such a block is supported at its ends, and lies in the same position which it had when it grew, it bends under a weight, just as a beam would (Fig. 49, A). If it is turned on its edge and placed so that the layers which were horizontal are now vertical, and their plane is parallel to the line joining the supports (Fig. 49, B), then the block yields very little indeed. If the planes that

THE NATURE OF CRYSTALS

were horizontal are perpendicular to the line joining the support they slide on one another, and the ice block is altered in shape (Fig. 49, C). If under pressure and local melting a few molecules are set sufficiently free to move as a liquid into a new place, they will, as in the case of the wire, readily join on to the ice structure on either side, simply because a place is always waiting for them. But we can look on the effect in the general sense as due to the movement of the planes over one another.

It is curious to see with what readiness pieces of ice join together. If we rest one fairly flat piece

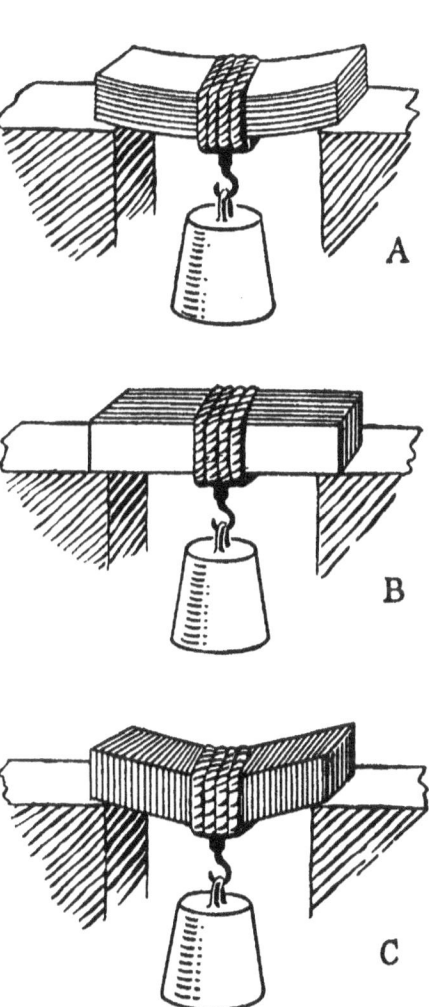

FIG. 49.—A set of planks arranged as in A would bend under a weight. Set up on edge as in B, they would bend far less. If arranged as in C, stuck together by some very viscous substance, they would yield gradually and continuously.

on another for a few moments, we can, keeping hold of the latter piece, turn the pair upside down, and the added piece does not fall. When two pieces of ice are held together under water, even warm water, they join together.

We may now go back to the consideration of the peculiar chain molecules of carbon atoms which, from want of time, we were obliged to leave over from the last lecture. When we considered the structure of the diamond, we saw that there was a certain arrangement of the carbon atoms which was found everywhere within it. It was an arrangement of six atoms in the form of a ring. We saw that a similar arrangement formed the basis of the so-called benzene ring, which is a molecule formed by fringing the six-sided carbon ring with six hydrogen atoms; and that a very large number of other important molecules were founded on the same arrangement, the hydrogen atoms being replaced by various other atoms or groups of atoms. The study of these molecules is the purpose of one of the great branches of organic chemistry. The molecules form substances which are called " aromatic," because many of them have a fragrant smell.

There is a second great branch of organic chemistry, which deals with substances of a different kind. They are called " aliphatic," the word implying that they are well represented by oils and fats. The chemist has been able to prove that in this case the molecule is formed of a chain of carbon atoms, to which various atoms, particularly hydrogens, may be attached along its length and at its end. The ring was obvious in the diamond structure. It seems, from recent experiments, that we may find the chain also in the diamond; so that the diamond contains the essentials of both the great branches.

We considered a few examples of the ring in the last lecture, but left the chain until to-day. The chain is formed of any number of links, each of which, in general, is made out of one atom of carbon and two atoms of hydrogen; and the ends are formed of various groups of atoms, of which some are very common and give to the chain well-known characteristics. In the simplest case the ends are formed of hydrogen atoms, and we have then the hydrocarbon or paraffin molecule. The symbol of pentane, for example, is written by the chemist as follows :—

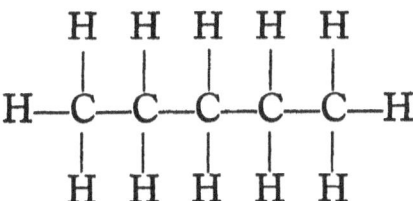

Pentane is an inflammable liquid used in standard

lamps—that is to say, lamps which serve as a standard of comparison for other lamps, because they burn with a steady and constant flame. The diagram is intended to represent the way in which the various atoms are attached to one another. Each carbon is joined to four other atoms. The carbon atom cannot link up closely to more than four, so that the molecule cannot be added to without first breaking it somewhere. It is said to be saturated. In the diagram it is represented as lying altogether in one plane, partly because of convenience of drawing, partly because so little is known of its actual arrangement. One of the objects of the X-ray analysis is to determine the relative positions of the atoms in a molecule more accurately than has been possible hitherto, and to measure the linear dimensions. In the case of these long-chain molecules, the X-rays have recently had an unexpected success. In order to express this additional knowledge, we really need a model or a sketch in perspective; a model of the probable form of the pentane molecule is shown in Plate XXI A.

Many members of the paraffin series are found mixed together in petroleum wells. They are inflammable, because they readily break up under

PLATE XXI.

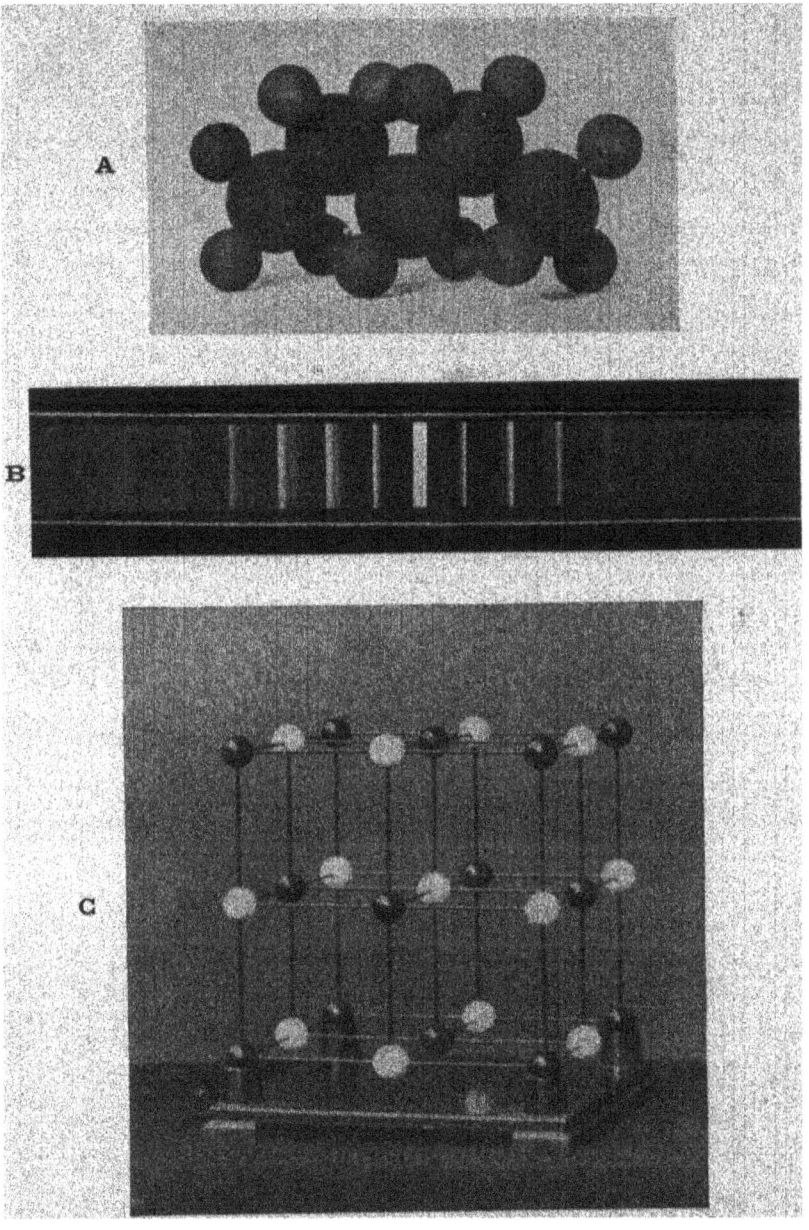

A. Model of a hydrogen chain, pentane, containing five carbon atoms. The larger balls represent carbon atoms, the smaller hydrogens.
B. An X-ray spectrum of the hydrocarbon containing 18 carbons obtained by the method shown in Fig. 52. (Muller.)
C. The model shows the arrangement of the sodium and chlorine atoms in rock-salt: the dark balls represent sodium, the white chlorine, or vice versa. Only *arrangement* is shown: there is no attempt to show the size or shape of the atom.

THE NATURE OF CRYSTALS 187

the proper stimulus in the presence of oxygen, and the atoms rush into fresh combinations, developing great heat in doing so. The shortest member of the series contains only one link. It is a gas, called methane or marsh gas, represented thus :—

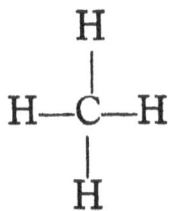

It bubbles up from stagnant water containing vegetable matter in decay. As the chain grows longer, the substance holds together better. Pentane, with five links, is a liquid at ordinary temperatures and boils at 36° C.; pentadecane, with fifteen links, boils at 257° C., while pentacosane, with twenty-five links, is solid at ordinary temperatures and melts at 54° C. The long molecules are supposed to have a tendency to lie side by side, like matches in a box; we shall see that this view is strongly supported by the X-ray results. It may, therefore, be expected that the longer they are, the greater the forces required to tear them apart; so that for this reason alone the longer the chain the higher its boiling point and melting point. As a class they have no strong hold on each other: the boiling and melting points are low. The cloak of hydrogens with which they are covered seems to hinder their association with other molecules such as those of acids. In fact, the word paraffin is derived from two Latin words meaning "little" and "affinity." But, as I have already said, they join up very readily with oxygen under the proper circumstances.

The behaviour of these chains is greatly altered if we take off an end group and put on a different one. By substituting for one of the end hydrogens a certain group, containing a carbon, two oxygens and a hydrogen, we get another highly important series of compounds called the "fatty acids." The group is known as the carboxyl group. Here again the chain may be of any length. When there is only one carbon in it, the chemist represents it thus:—

$$H-C\begin{smallmatrix}\diagup O \\ \diagdown O \diagdown H,\end{smallmatrix}$$

meaning that of the four bonds which carbon can exert, drawing four other atoms to itself, one goes to a hydrogen, another to an oxygen which carries a hydrogen, and two go to a separate oxygen, binding it very tightly. This substance is formic

THE NATURE OF CRYSTALS 189

acid, which is secreted by ants, and has a very irritating action on the skin, as we all know. When a fresh link is added to the chain, we have acetic acid, which gives acidity to vinegar; in fact, the name is derived from the Latin word for vinegar. The formula is now:—

$$\text{H}-\underset{\underset{\text{H}}{|}}{\overset{\overset{\text{H}}{|}}{\text{C}}}-\text{C}\underset{\text{O}-\text{H}}{\overset{\text{O}}{\diagup\diagdown}}$$

Butyric acid has four carbons; it is the substance that gives to rancid butter its peculiar taste and smell. Lauric acid has twelve carbons, and is found in laurel oil and cocoanut oil. Myristic acid has fourteen, and is found in the butters of mace and nutmeg. All these are liquids. Palmitic acid, found in palm oil, has sixteen, and stearic has eighteen. The last two are solids at ordinary temperatures. They are used in the manufacture of stearine candles, and, slightly modified, are the most important constituents of animal fat.

The alcohols constitute another of these chain series. They are formed from the paraffins by taking off a hydrogen from one end and replacing it by an oxygen and a hydrogen in combination. Thus:—

$$\begin{array}{c} \text{H} \quad \text{H} \\ | \quad | \\ \text{H—C—C—O—H} \\ | \quad | \\ \text{H} \quad \text{H} \end{array}$$

is the ordinary alcohol.

And so we may go on, describing an immense number of substances, all consisting of links of CH_2, with varying terminations. Sometimes one or more hydrogens are taken off the side of the chain and replaced by other atoms or atom groups; sometimes there are further complications. There is a fascination in the simplicity of the general principle and in the wonderful variety and influence of detail. Why should different plants or different animals, or different members of the same plant or animal, contain these carbon chains of different lengths, on which their own growth and properties and characteristics greatly depend? Of course, the whole effect rests, in the first place, on the properties of the carbon atom, and it is that which gives a peculiar interest to the crystal forms of carbon, diamond and graphite.

We may look again at the diamond model and ask ourselves whether we can see any skeleton

THE NATURE OF CRYSTALS 191

form of the chain, just as we saw the skeleton of the ring. The model (Plate XIV A) shows that it can be cut into chains of any length and of this form :—

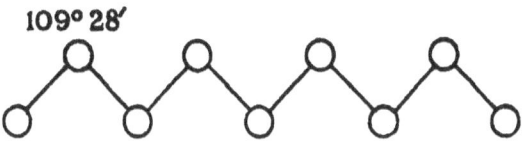

FIG. 50.—Chain from diamond.

in which the angle that recurs at every bend can be calculated to be 109° 28'. We might suppose this to be a simple form of the chain. We are only speculating, of course, trying to imagine possible solutions of our problems, which we may put to the test of experiment, and even when we seem to have a success, not counting too much upon it. If this were the chain, two hydrogens would naturally be attached to each carbon at points which, with the two points of attachment of its carbon neighbours, would make four points symmetrically arranged, like the four points at which each carbon atom is attached to its four neighbours in the diamond, as in Plate XXI A. This picture goes more into details than the form of illustration generally employed by the chemist ; the latter is merely a representation on the flat, our new figure is in three dimensions. And no doubt the true figure is in three dimensions. The chemist has not drawn it so hitherto, because he has had no direct evidence as to how he ought to do it. We are trying to go one stage further; with some hesitation, because we are not perfect in the interpretation of our new methods, though very hopeful as to their value to us in the end.

In the last year or two we have been able to make accurate measurements of the lengths of the chain molecules by means of the X-rays. The discovery of the method arose from a curious accident. A certain crystal was under examination by X-rays, and because it was liable to suffer rapid deterioration from the moisture of the air, it was covered over with a thin layer of the solid paraffin which is generally used in laboratories as an electric insulator. Certain reflections of the X-rays were found which could not be reconciled with what was known. It was found that they were due to the paraffin. The commercial paraffin is a mixture of several of the fatty acid chains, and is not suitable for accurate experiment. It happened, however, that a certain enthusiastic student of organic chemistry, Dr. Le Sueur, had prepared a great number of these chain substances in a pure state, and these were fortunately available. Those and many

THE NATURE OF CRYSTALS 193

others have now been examined, with very interesting and, on the whole, simple results.

The particular method is a good example of the way in which the X-rays can be used. A little of the solid substance is put on a piece of glass and pressed flat : we will consider the significance of the pressing in a moment. The substance is now, as it turns out, in layers parallel to the glass. The molecules in each layer are more or less perpendicular to it and are linked together side by side. They may be represented as in Fig. 51, in which three layers are drawn. Each layer is perhaps a fifty-millionth of an inch thick, and the thickness is proportional to the length of the molecule. When a beam of X-rays is passed through such a sheet, composed of layers, a little is reflected by each layer, just as would happen in the case of a beam of light passing though a pile of glass plates. The principle of the experiment has already been described on p. 140. Suppose S is the source of the X-rays, and P_1P_1 is the glass plate with its layers upon it. When the X-ray beam along SC falls on the plate at the proper angle, the reflection from the different layers are all in step

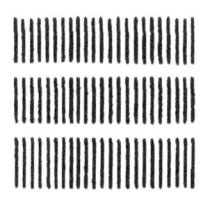

FIG. 51 —Diagrammatic arrangement of the molecules in the layers of a substance like stearic acid, or a hydrocarbon such as pentane.

o

and the reflection is strong. We may imagine the reflected ray going off on the line CR_1, and making its mark at R_1 on the photographic plate DD. If the plate is then turned round about the vertical line through C—the figure shows the experiment in plan—reflection as a whole ceases, because the separate reflections from the various layers get out of step and destroy each other. But when the plate has been turned sufficiently, another

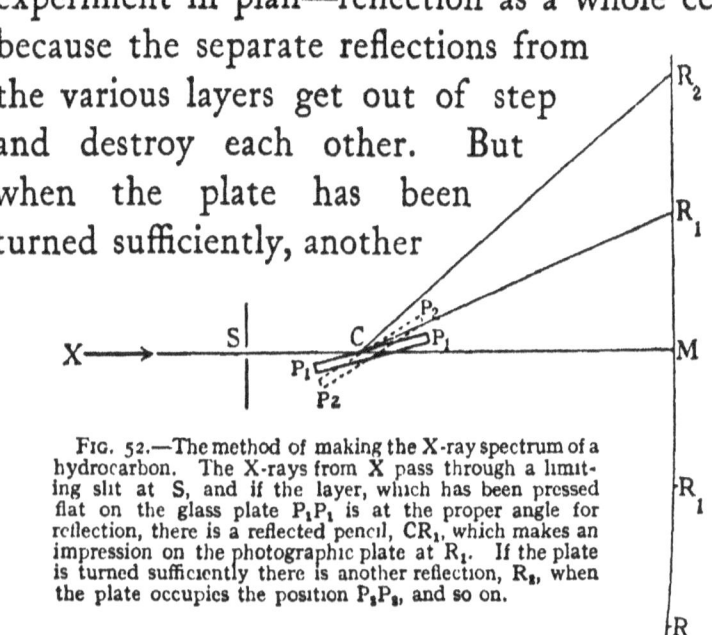

FIG. 52.—The method of making the X-ray spectrum of a hydrocarbon. The X-rays from X pass through a limiting slit at S, and if the layer, which has been pressed flat on the glass plate P_1P_1 is at the proper angle for reflection, there is a reflected pencil, CR_1, which makes an impression on the photographic plate at R_1. If the plate is turned sufficiently there is another reflection, R_2, when the plate occupies the position P_2P_2, and so on.

general reflection appears, because the reflections from the different layers have got into step again. The first general reflection comes when the particular reflection from one layer is *one* wave-length behind or in advance of the reflection from the layers on either side of it; the next when there is a difference of *two* wavelengths, and so on. Consequently the photo-

THE NATURE OF CRYSTALS 195

graphic plate when it is developed shows a whole series of such general reflections. Usually the plate is turned so as to throw reflections both above and below the line (Fig. 52). A central mark M is due to the direct action of the X-rays —this part of the plate is usually shielded, so that the direct action is not too strong—and all the different orders of reflection appear on either side. An actual example showing the reflection of a paraffin of 18 carbons is shown in Plate XXI B. It was obtained by Dr. Müller. It will be seen that the reflections are very well marked. It is possible to measure their distance apart with accuracy, and from this we calculate the thickness of one of the layers in the reflecting material. We cannot be quite sure that the molecules stand upright and perpendicular to the layer, but we have good grounds for supposing so, which we need not enter into here. We find that the length of the chain increases with perfect regularity as carbon links are added to it. We actually find that many of them have exactly the length we should expect if they were as represented in Fig. 50.

The whole series of experiments of this kind bears out the idea that the chemist has formed as to the shape of these molecules : his representation has been wonderfully correct. The X-rays have given precision to the idea, suggesting also that the molecule must be drawn in three dimensions, and at the same time measuring the length. I may add that the sideways dimensions can be measured also.

We may now go back to the curious point that we get much better X-ray reflections if the material is pressed on to the glass plate. It seems likely that it naturally forms flakes, and in each flake the molecules are perpendicular to the flake. They join together side by side, as I have already said, and hold together much better in this union than one flake holds to another. This last linking is affected by the ties at the ends of the molecules, and these are much weaker. It is exactly the same effect as we found in graphite, where flakes held together strongly as flakes, but slid easily on one another. It is this that gives the greasy, slippery feeling both to the greases and fats and to graphite. When pressure is applied to the material, the layers are squeezed flat, just as when graphite is rubbed on a surface, and the X-ray reflections are good because the layers are made to lie regularly. When the material is melted and cooled again, the layers are broken up, and though, no doubt, they are formed again, they lie irregularly; the X-ray reflection is then poor. We find the

THE NATURE OF CRYSTALS 197

same effect in the case of gold leaf, as we shall see in the next lecture.

There is another curious property of the long-chain molecules which is worth our consideration. The paraffin chain has hydrogens at both ends. Each flake is one molecule thick. But in the case of the fatty acids (p. 188), the X-rays show that there are two molecules in the layer, end to end. This is, indeed, to be expected, because it is known that a carboxyl group has a tendency to join up with another of its own kind. Consequently the chains attach themselves together in pairs, forming a chain of double length, the ends of which are hydrogens; the two carboxyl groups are in the centre. This result is obtained from the X-ray measurements. Here again the X-rays confirm a chemical conclusion and throw a fresh light upon it.

There is a type of crystal structure which, differing entirely from those that we have considered already, is of such great importance that we must not pass it by. The crystals of ordinary salt are good examples.

Sometimes, as we have already seen, a molecule is formed from two atoms, of which one, being greedy for an additional electron, has satisfied itself at the expense of the other atom. The latter, before the transference, has held one electron in a loose binding. For example, chlorine has seventeen electrons: two in an innermost shell or coating, and eight in the next shell. In the outer shell there are seven, and the chlorine atom exerts a great force, tending to complete the shell, which when full contains eight. It will then present the external appearance of argon. Sodium has eleven electrons normally: two in the innermost shell and eight in the next, but only one in the outer shell instead of the seven in chlorine. The sodium atom has no tight hold on this odd electron, so the chlorine takes it. The sodium atom then has the external appearance of a neon atom. (See p. 76.)

The two atoms are now charged electrically; the chlorine is negative, because it has one negative charge over and above its proper number, and the sodium is positive, because it has one too few. The governing principle in the growth of the crystal is the attempt on the part of the atoms to satisfy as fully as possible the mutual attraction of the positive sodiums and the negative chlorines. The system of packing which Nature adopts is that in which each chlorine is surrounded by six sodiums and vice versa. It is shown in Plate XXI C. It is very simple—a cubic arrangement in which

THE NATURE OF CRYSTALS 199

each of the lines of atoms that are parallel to the edges consists of sodium and chlorine atoms alternately. The white balls may represent chlorine and the black sodium, or vice versa. It is because of this arrangement that salt crystallises from brine in cubic form. The crystals are not necessarily cubes, but are rectangular blocks, all faces of which are of the same type. The frequent differences between their sizes and appearances are merely accidents of growth.

Very many crystals are built on this principle : in particular all the salts of the metals, in which the metal has lost one or more electrons, and the remainder of the molecule, as a group, has gained them. The resulting structure is not always so simple as that of salt, because, for instance, the group may be more irregular in outline than the single chlorine. In calcite, the metal atom calcium loses two electrons to the group CO_3, and the result is the rhomb of Iceland spar. It is still true that each metal atom is surrounded by six negatively charged bodies, and each of the latter by six metal atoms; the crystal is no longer rectangular, because the CO_3 group is not round.

LECTURE VI

THE NATURE OF CRYSTALS: METALS

THE use of metals has been one of the great factors in the development of the activities of the human race. The beginning of the story is so far back in the ages that we can only make guesses as to how men first made metal tools and weapons. Perhaps copper was picked up in its native state, and its weight suggested its usefulness in a fight. Copper is too soft to take a cutting edge, and it may not have been very long before it was found that there was an alloy of copper and tin which was far harder and more serviceable than copper alone. Perhaps there was tin in the stones of which the copper smelting furnace was built, perhaps copper and tin occurred together in the same mineral. And so the age of bronze set in. Iron came later, of course. From that time to this there have been workers of metal: important members of the human community. We have but to think of the magnitude of the metal industry in this country alone,

THE NATURE OF CRYSTALS

to realise how great a part the metals play in the life of the world.

In all these thousands of years a vast body of experience has been gained. Some of it is in books, some of it is still a tradition handed down by the skilled workman to the apprentice. There is even a sense of the nature, or condition, or property of a metal which cannot be put into words, and is only taught by example to such as have the power to understand. Nor is this any trifling matter: the whole movement of trade and the welfare of a nation may rest upon it.

On the other hand, the properties of the metals must depend, in the first place, on the properties of the individual atoms, and, in the second place, on the atomic arrangement, which is in effect the state of crystallisation. In the very centres of the metal industries it has been realised of recent years that the scientific observer with his microscope can bring some system into the mass of disordered knowledge, and can improve the quality of the manufacture and the certainty of its production. Yet, as I have said already, the microscope can only go to a certain length: it stops far short of the point which we must reach if we are to understand how the atoms are acting so as to give the various materials their specific properties.

It can show the existence of the separate crystals in the metal, but not the arrangement of the atoms in the crystals (Plates XXII, XXIII). In the X-rays we find a new hope: indeed it is more than a hope. We may be sure that the intimate knowledge which they give us will in the end throw a flood of light upon the inner meaning and purpose of all the complex properties of metals. It may be a long time before the new movement will become great and obvious. The experience of thousands of years has to be caught up with and explained. It is quite otherwise with such a subject as electrical engineering, or wireless telephony, which is a branch of it. Here the whole process is rooted in the work of the physics laboratory, and development has been directed by knowledge and anticipation. The worker in metals has been guided through the ages by trial and error, by experiment with little knowledge to guide it. It is a very slow process; but it has been going on a long time, and its findings command respect. They must be studied very carefully in the new light which the X-rays give us.

Already we begin to find explanations, as we may call them, of some of the properties of the metals. They depend upon the crystalline structure, as we might have expected. Sometimes the crystals

PLATE XXII.

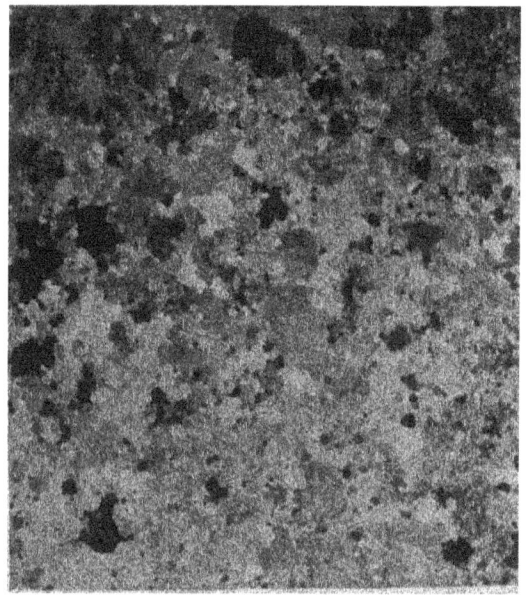

Two photographs of aluminium: the surface has been prepared so as to show the different crystals. The crystals scatter the incident light differently because they are set in different ways, and the surfaces exposed by treatment are therefore different in nature. In one figure the scale has been reduced somewhat from the natural size, in the other considerably enlarged.

(From a paper by Carpenter and Elam, read before the Institute of Metals, Sept. 1920.)

PLATE XXIII

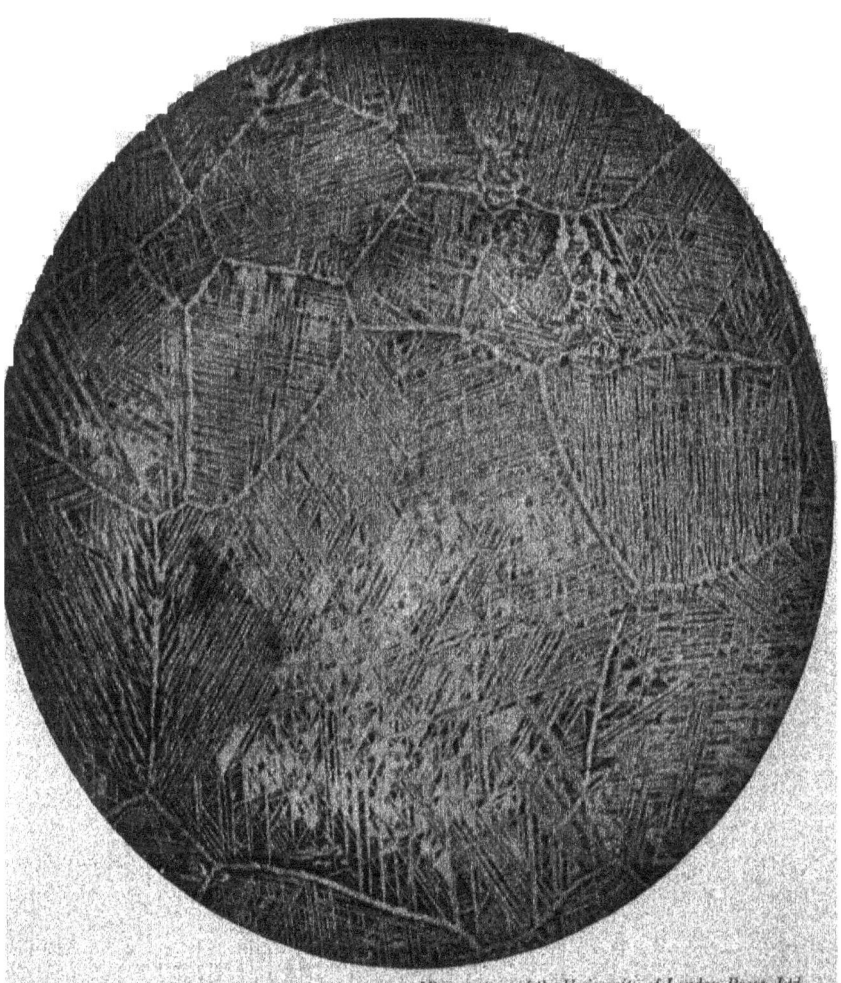

[*By courtesy of the University of London Press, Ltd.*

The photograph shows the irregular outline of the crystal grains in a sample of steel, and, in addition, a criss-crossing of lines within each grain, known as "Widmanstätten lines." These last are due to the fact that the polishing tool has cut across the "atom layers," in much the same way as polishing cuts across layers of mother of pearl.

(From Belaiew's "Crystallisation of Metals.")

THE NATURE OF CRYSTALS

are to be seen by the naked eye; sometimes they become obvious when the surface is properly prepared and placed under the microscope. But the easiest and most complete way of discovering them is by means of the X-rays, with their fineness of vision.

The structures of almost all the metal crystals have been determined by the X-rays, and it appears that they are usually very simple. For instance, the atoms of gold, silver, copper and aluminium are put together like the piles of round shot that used to stand beside the guns of a hundred years ago.

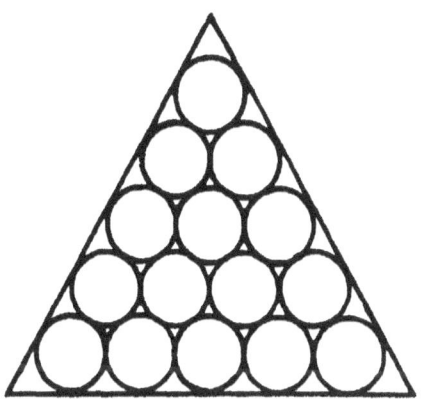

FIG. 53.—A close-packed arrangement of balls in one layer.

It is worth while to look a little carefully into this arrangement, although we are really repeating the comparison (p. 176) between the structures of ice and diamond. Suppose we put together a number of balls into the triangular arrangement of Fig. 53, and surround them by a triangular guard, as shown, just as balls are packed together for playing snooker on the billiard table.

We lay on these another layer, forming a triangle a little smaller than the first, and again other layers until the triangular pyramid is finished (Plate XXIV B). Obviously there can be no closer method of packing round balls together. Now if we look into the arrangement of the layers one above another, we find that the balls in any layer are exactly over the balls in the next layer but *two*. In the absence of a model this effect may be realised by the help of Fig. 54. The crosses represent the centres of the balls in a certain layer, the circles the centres in the next layer, and the black spots the centres in the third. The centres in the fourth will be over the crosses, in the fifth over the circles, and in the sixth over the spots, and so on.

When balls are arranged in this way, it is possible to cut cubes out of the assembly, as in Plate XXV A. It is always a surprise when this fact is first realised, but it is well to understand the cause of it, because so many crystals are made up of atoms piled together in this way, and they so often grow as cubes or in some way show their close connection with the cubic form.

Now if, when we have laid down two layers and come to the arrangement of the third, we place it so that each ball is exactly over a ball in

PLATE XXIV.

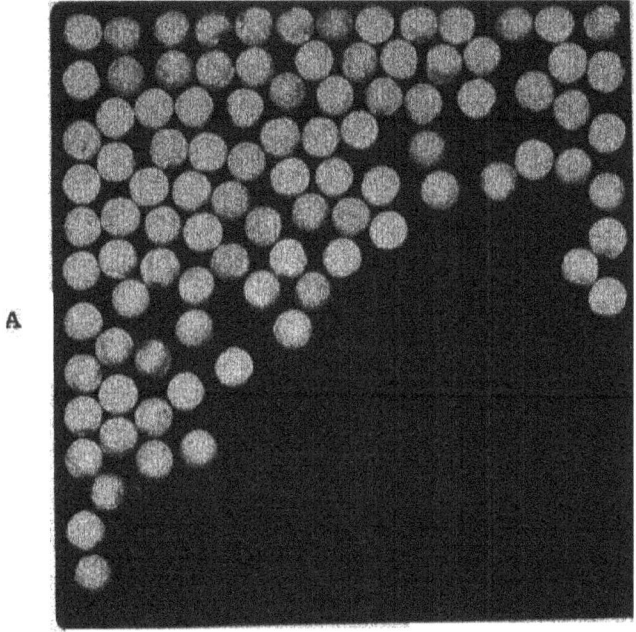

A. Small groups of shot are in close packing, and there are irregular gaps between the groups.
B. A pyramid, built by the super-position of layers like that of Fig. 53.

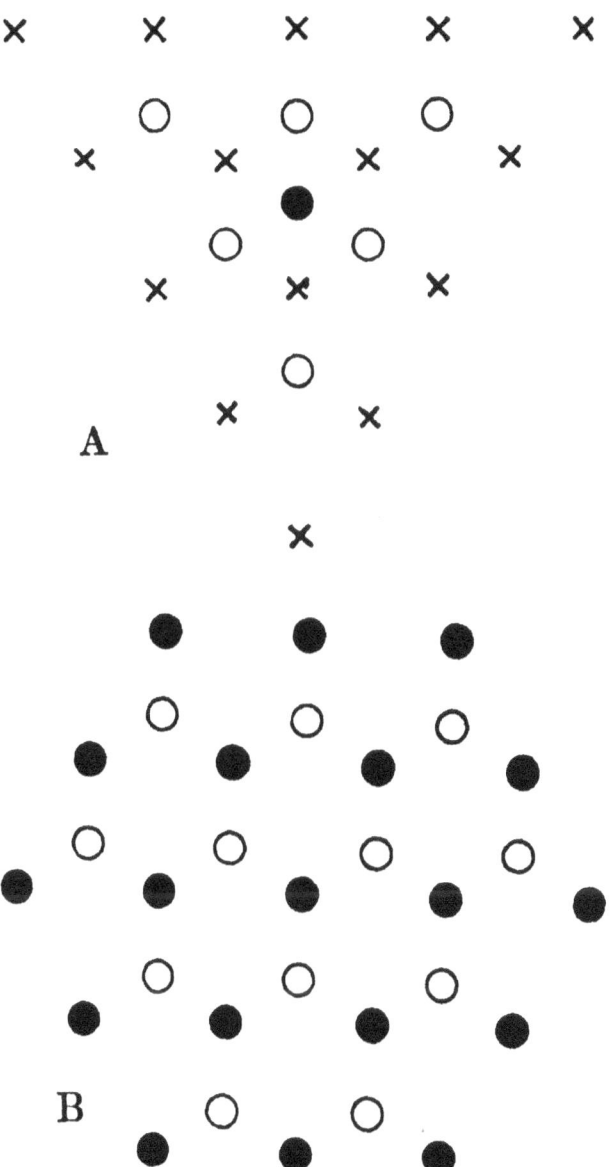

Fig. 54.—In A is shown the arrangement of the layers as seen by an observer looking along a diagonal of the cube of Plate XXV A. The black spot represents the ball at the corner. The small circles represent the six balls in the next layer, and the crosses the fifteen in the next layer. In B the arrangement is as seen by an observer looking down on Plate XXV B from above. The nineteen black spots represent the balls in the top layer, and the twelve small circles the balls in the next layer. The third layer is like the first, the fourth like the second, and so on. The repetition is after every second layer: in A it is after every third.

the first layer, which arrangement is the only alternative to the one we chose before, we have another way of packing the balls which is as compact as the other. In this case, the balls in any layer are exactly over the balls in the *next layer but one*, and Fig. 54, A, will be replaced by Fig. 54, B, and the arrangement of Plate XXV A by that of XXV B. This arrangement will not stand up now without containing walls, if we are to have a reasonable number of balls in the model; we must pin them together in some way. When we look down on this model from above, we see six-sided tunnels running through it, and we do not see any arrangement of this kind when we look in any other direction. The model has a single axis in the vertical direction, and round that axis the arrangement is such that a crystal built on this plan would naturally form hexagonal columns.

In the case of the cube there are four ways of thinking of the arrangement of the layers; there is a layer perpendicular to each diagonal of the cube, and as a cube has four diagonals, there are four sets of layers. This does not mean that the atoms in any one layer are specially tied together in that layer; merely that one can sort out the atoms of the crystal into this kind of layer in four different ways.

PLATE XXV.

A.

B.

    A. Cubic packing.   **B.** Hexagonal packing.
(From Pope's "Modern Aspects of the Molecular Theory.")

A shows how balls are packed together to form a cube. It is exactly the same packing as in Plate XXIV B. The close-packed layers of Fig. 53 are horizontal in Plate XXIV B, and in A they are perpendicular to a diagonal of the cube.

B shows the other form of close packing. Each horizontal layer is a close-packed layer of Fig. 53.

THE NATURE OF CRYSTALS 207

Now it turns out that these layers are of very great importance in respect to the properties of the metal crystals built on the close-packed cubic plan. Gold, silver, copper, aluminium and other metals like them can be drawn into wires, rolled into sheets, and beaten into various shapes. They are, as we say, ductile, and their ductility is one of the characteristics that make them so useful. They can be bent and pulled into all sorts of convenient forms. It seems possible to make a metal flow like treacle. Gold can be hammered into leaves so thin that the metal in a sovereign will cover a large field; the others can be beaten nearly as thin. Cups and vessels of all sorts, chains and ornaments, and innumerable useful things are made by taking advantage of this singular property of ductility. The first thing that we should like the X-rays to explain for us more clearly, if we can make them do so, is that feature in their structure which accounts for this most valuable property. We should also like to understand the inner meaning of the hardening and other changes that are due to "cold-working," as it is called—that is to say, to hammering or straining the metal when it is cold. And what is annealing, the softening and relief from strain that heat brings about? Why are all these things so obvious in the case of a metal, while they do not appear in, for instance, diamond or rock salt or quartz?

Already we begin to see some little way into these difficult questions; and in particular we have found out something about the way in which the metal yields to a pull or any other strain, and have learnt that it has to do with the layers of which I have spoken.

A metal is rarely one whole crystal: it is in general an assemblage of crystals, pointing in all directions. Sometimes these crystals can be seen easily; sometimes the microscope is required to show them. Very often they are too small even for the microscope, and the X-rays alone can make them clear.

If we put a number of shot on a tray and let them all run together into a single layer by tilting the tray slightly (Plate XXIV A), we observe that there is a tendency for the shot to arrange themselves like the balls in Fig. 53. It will not often happen that all the shot will form *one* arrangement : there will be groups, each properly arranged in itself, but not correctly aligned with its neighbours. In just the same way there will be local arrangements among the atoms of a metal—in other words, there will be crystallisation in groups, larger or

THE NATURE OF CRYSTALS

smaller, the connection between the groups being somewhat irregular. We may observe at once that the connection between group and group is not necessarily any weaker than the connection between the atoms in any one group. Why this is so, it is difficult to say. We need not be surprised at it, because the ties between atoms are complicated things, imperfectly known to us, and we cannot predict accurately what will happen in every case. It is said that when gold is at a high temperature a fracture cuts through the crystals, but when the gold is cold it goes round them; and this will illustrate the complexity of the effect.

A block of one of these metals may reasonably be expected, therefore, to consist of a mass of crystals, large and small; and this is exactly what the X-rays show to be the case, even when the microscope fails because the crystals are too small for it to see.

Now when we take a single crystal and try to bend it or distort it, we find always that it gives finally through a slip along a plane: all that is on one side of the plane slipping with respect to all that is on the other. These planes are the planes we spoke of before—those that contain atoms arranged as in Fig. 53. A single metal crystal does not give way exactly in the direction in which it is pulled. If we had two blocks of glass, let us say, held together by grease as in Fig. 55, and pulled them, they would give along the plane between them. Naturally they will slide over one another on this plane rather than themselves be torn to pieces. In the case of a metal there is not merely one plane, but many planes, and many of them will be planes of sliding either together or one after another. We might represent the crystal by a set of lines as in Fig. 56 (a), which, if pulled in the direction of the arrows, would yield as in Fig. 56 (b). Often when a single metallic crystal has been stretched, we can see the marks on its surface which show the lines along which slip has taken place.

Professor Carpenter and

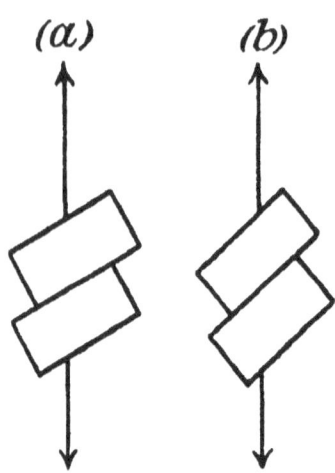

FIG. 55.—The two blocks are stuck together, but can slide over one another. When pulled they change in relative position from (a) to (b).

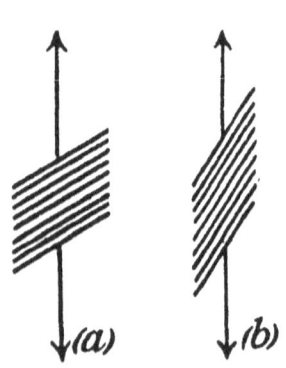

FIG. 56.—This figure represents in the form of a diagram the slipping on one another of the layers of the aluminium crystal.

PLATE XXVI.

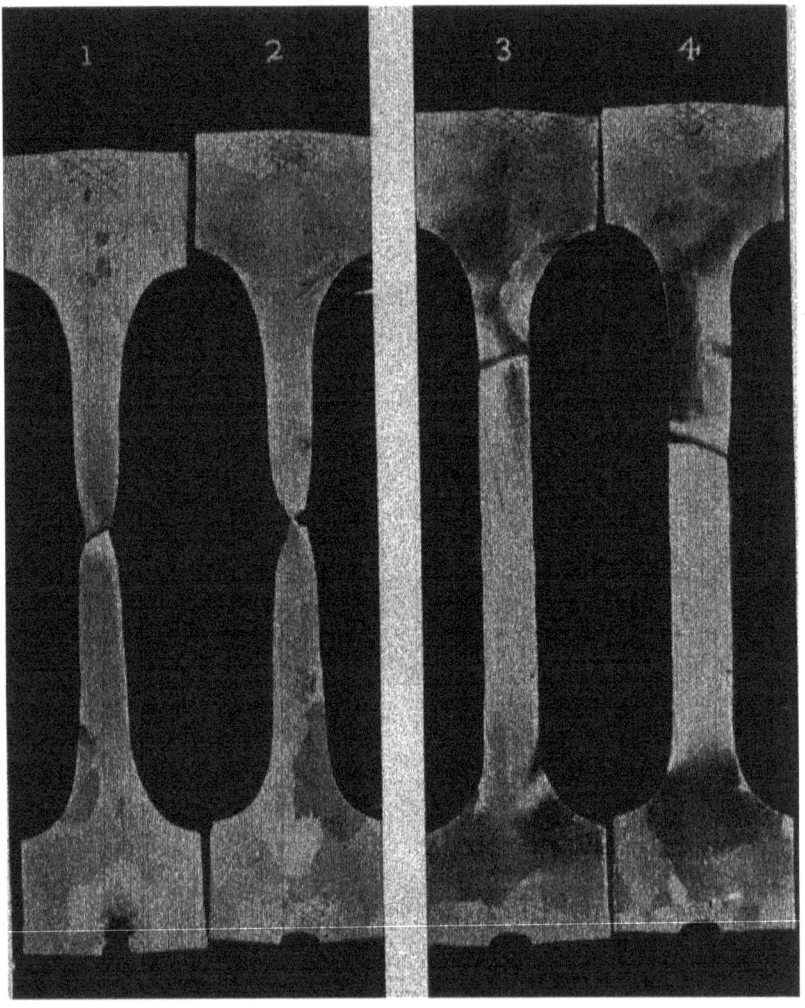

These photographs are due to Professor Carpenter and Miss Elam (*Proceedings of the Royal Society*, A., 100, p. 346). They show the yielding of aluminium under strain, the part finally giving way being a single large crystal in the narrower portion of the test piece. In (1) and (2) the slip planes are disposed—to the observer—like the layers of Fig. 56. The test piece has contracted sideways, and finally developed a waist, as the picture shows. There is no thinning from back to front. In (3) and (4) the reverse has taken place before the break: the width has remained the same, but the material has grown thinner (this cannot be seen in the photograph).

THE NATURE OF CRYSTALS

Miss Elam have shown recently some beautiful examples of this kind of effect in the case of large crystals of aluminium. An ordinary piece of the metal consists of a multitude of crystals pointing in all ways, as we have already understood to be the case. By a somewhat complicated process of heating and stretching, the many small crystals can all be made to line up and form a small number of large crystals, just as we might imagine that by shaking or tapping the tray of shot shown in Plate XXIV A in some way, to be found out by experience, we could get all the minor regular groupings merged into one large one.

The pieces chosen for experiment were of a form often used for pieces to be tested for their resistance to pull; the form is shown in Plate XXVI; the original length of each piece is 8 inches. The broad ends are intended to be gripped by the jaws of the machine that is to stretch the piece; the narrower part is that which is to give way, and to show by the way in which it does so, and the pull that is exerted, the capacity of the metal to resist the forces that would strain it.

When one of the test pieces so treated is put into the testing machine and pulled, it gives way in a curious fashion, which differs for different specimens (Plate XXVI, 1 to 4). Sometimes the width of the piece remains the same, and it thins out gradually as the test piece lengthens under the pull: it may grow longer by several inches before it gives way. Sometimes the thickness remains the same, and the piece shrinks sideways, developing a waist which finally is the place of breaking. At other times, again, there are more curious changes still. These pieces have been examined by the X-rays, and it turns out that the nature of the yield depends entirely on the way in which the large crystals are set towards the line of pull. The metal gives way along the plane of slip. If, for example, the crystal is so set—and there is no telling during the heat and strain treatment how the forming crystal will lie—that the layers of which we have spoken are as in Fig. 56, then stretching will make the piece draw in sideways.

Sometimes the direction in which the crystal gives way depends on a more complicated use of two sets of slip planes alternately. When the crystal might slip on more than one set of planes, it is apt to choose the one which is more nearly perpendicular to the line of pull. We can imagine that this is so because a slip means a riding of one set of atoms over another, and the motion would be helped by a force tending to pull one layer away from the other. If we had a solid body

THE NATURE OF CRYSTALS

made up of a row of balls like the top layer in Fig. 57, and it rested on a similar row like the bottom layer, it might be easier to drag the top layer over the bottom if the line of pull were along P rather than along Q. Since (see Fig. 55) the pull always tends to bring the plane of slip

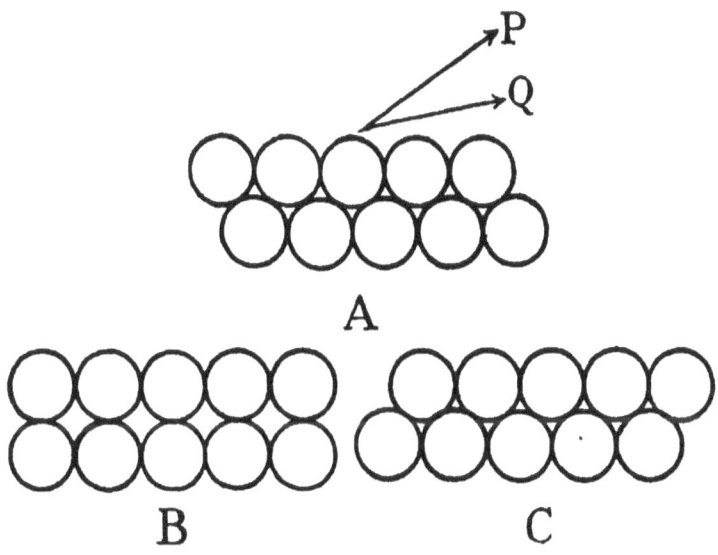

Fig. 57.—The top layer, as a unit, might be more easily pulled through from position A, through B, to C, if the pull were along P than if it were along Q.

more nearly into its own line, there arises a sort of see-saw action : the crystal slips along one set of planes until the set comes too nearly into line with the pull, and then along another. In the end the line of pull bisects the angle between the two sets. The balance is often shown in the shape of the broken ends ; in Plate XXVI, 3, for example, there is a kind of knife-edge at the point of rupture. The two sides of the edge are parallel to two different sets of slip planes, and are equally inclined to the line of the pull which finally tore the metal in two.

In the case of the aluminium, the yield is so easy that a sheet of some thickness, when composed of a single crystal, can be bent quite easily by one's fingers. An ordinary piece of aluminium sheet is quite stiff, however, and the explanation of the difference is that, when there are crystals pointing in all directions, there are some ready to take and bear the strain, no matter from what direction it comes. The strength of a chain is that of its weakest link, and the weak part of a crystal is its slip plane. This is a point of extraordinary importance in the manufacture of metal, though it is often linked up with so many others that its special effect is difficult to sort out from the rest. Many factors go to the design of steel, let us say, for some given purpose; but one of them is certainly the degree of fineness of the crystal grains of which it is composed. Fineness and uniformity of size both contribute to the toughness of steel and its quality generally.

When the single crystal of aluminium gives way along a layer, we may suppose there is a moment

THE NATURE OF CRYSTALS

when the one set of atoms is riding over the other, followed by a drop into place again : A goes through B into C (Fig. 57). When the latter case is reached, the close-packed arrangement is resumed. The metal is still a crystal. Now, as we know, the regular crystalline arrangement is the natural one, and so the substance slips easily from one natural arrangement to another, adjusting itself to the pull or other strain by doing so. No doubt this is one of the causes, and a very important cause, of ductility.

But why does the metal often become harder when it is beaten? And what happens to it when it is annealed? Perhaps we are guided towards an answer by considering what happens to gold when it is beaten into leaf and subsequently heated. Gold leaf is very thin, as we have seen. It is even transparent, but it absorbs part of the spectrum of light that passes through it, allowing a greenish light to filter through. It is yellow when viewed by reflected light, as we know. It is very curious that when it has been heated to a dull red heat it becomes permanently transparent, and white by reflected light. Faraday was very interested in this fact; he suggested as a partial explanation that the thin layer of gold broke up, the metal gathering itself together in little heaps, and that the light went through the holes that were left. Sir George Beilby has made many experiments, and added considerably to the information we have in regard to the behaviour of this and other substances when heated in the same way. If there are holes in the heated leaf, they are exceedingly small, he says, beyond the power of the microscope to see. Now the X-rays have something to say on this point. When gold leaf is examined by their aid, it is found that it consists of masses of cubic crystals of gold all lying with faces parallel to the leaf. They are not necessarily cubes, of course. They consist, like ordinary salt, which is cubic, of rectangular blocks of all sizes. They must be exceedingly thin blocks, and no doubt their thickness is far less than their width or length. When the leaf has been heated, the blocks are piled up anyhow: perhaps gathered together to some extent in heaps, as Faraday supposed, even if they are too small to be seen by the microscope; and perhaps this is the reason why gold and silver leaf become transparent when heated. Why gold should be green when looked through is a mystery. But we do see that the beating of the gold has spread out the crystal blocks so that they all lie with one face in the leaf surface, and that heat has destroyed

THE NATURE OF CRYSTALS 217

this amount of regularity of arrangement. When the heated gold leaf is pressed with a body having a smooth, hard surface, such as an agate, it goes back to the other condition: as we might expect, since the pressure would force the blocks once more into the flat. In both cases the metal is crystalline, but there is more arrangement in the usual than in the annealed form of the gold leaf. The same effect is found with silver. To show it in the case of copper it would be necessary to carry out the experiment under such circumstances that the air could not act on the metal. When copper is heated in the open, a film of copper oxide quickly forms all over it, an action which also can be followed by the X-rays. We often see this tarnish form slowly on copper even when no heat is applied. But it is easy to show by X-rays that in copper foil there is the same arrangement of the crystal block as in the case of the gold leaf. On the other hand, a block of ordinary copper shows no such arrangement; the crystals are arranged anyhow.

The hardening of these metals by cold working is, therefore, due in some way to the fact that they are put into a state of strain by the rearrangement of the crystals which the X-rays show; annealing is the release of this strain and the destruction of the arrangement. As to why this is so, we are still very ignorant: we can simply be satisfied that we have made one step forward.

It is worth noting that, in general, when a metal has been thrown into a state of strain in this way, it is more readily subject to the action of chemicals, as we might expect. It is not so well settled into what we may call a comfortable condition.

We ought now to go on to the consideration of other peculiarities possessed by metals, since we may expect them all to be due to more or less the same causes and we must study them all together. Two of their most remarkable properties lie in their powers of conducting heat and electricity. We all know how quickly heat spreads through a metal: we might be inclined to say that a metal could be identified by its possession of that property. We all know, too, how metals, especially copper, are used as conductors of electric current.

Going back to our first consideration of the nature of the atoms, and of the differences between the various atoms, we find at once a feature which on the whole seems capable of giving us a satisfactory explanation of their conducting powers; no doubt, too, it has much to do with their crystal-

THE NATURE OF CRYSTALS 219

line structure and their ductility. The atoms of the metals always have one or more electrons, which are lightly held. For instance, sodium has eleven electrons; two of these are very close to the nucleus, eight more form a very strongly held system round the first two. The odd electron belongs to an outer system altogether, which becomes filled up as we go from sodium to magnesium with two in the outermost system, aluminium with three, and so on. This odd electron is not held tightly. When it is stripped off for any reason, the atom is outwardly reduced to the form of the unsociable atom "neon," except that as a whole it carries a positive electric charge due to the want of balance on loss of an electron. An aluminium crystal is an assemblage of spheres like neon, all in close packing, as explained, and all the odd electrons are more or less free to move about in the structure. It must be said, however, that this picture is doubtless much too crude to be the whole truth; there must be much more in the design of which as yet we know nothing. Yet it must be right to a certain extent. We see at once why metals are conductors of electricity: it is because the electrons, the fundamental charges of negative electricity, can move about so easily. When a current of electricity runs along a metal wire, it is the electrons that make the flowing stream. It is curious that they must move, being negatively charged, in the opposite direction to that in which the so-called current of electricity is always imagined to flow. It was always a matter of words, this talk of a flowing current of electricity. It is quite a new discovery that anything moves at all, and we need not be surprised that the real direction of flow is opposite to that which had been supposed.

So we must think of the battery or the dynamo, not as manufacturing electricity, but as sending round a circuit a stream of the electrons that are already there and are more or less free to move. Just so the engine in a factory makes a leather belt continually travel round a certain circuit; but the engine does not manufacture leather.

When a metal is heated, the contained electrons dance more quickly to and fro, and may break away into the open. Electrons are pouring in a continuous stream from the hot wire in the " valve " of wireless telephony, and the outpouring is necessary to the action of the valve.

The electrons do not move so easily in a metal when it is hot as when it is cold. Here again it is easy to imagine how this may be. We can see

THE NATURE OF CRYSTALS

that the electrons will have more difficulty in threading their way among the atoms of the metal if through heat the latter are moving to and fro and getting in their road. It is much more difficult to explain the strange fact, discovered at Leiden by Kamerlingh Onnes, that some substances when their temperature has been lowered to a certain very low point—a point which differs for different metals—offer no resistance at all to the movement of the electrons, so that a current once started will keep on running for days before it finally fades away, the metal being kept continuously at this extremely low temperature.

The electrons must to some extent contribute to the capacity of a metal for conveying heat as well as electricity, because the electrons at the hot end of a metal bar must pass on some of their excessive energy to the electrons at the cold end.

Thus the presence of electrons in the metal, able to move with some freedom among the atoms of the structure, gives a very good reason why the metal conducts both heat and electricity. Of course it is only a rough picture that we have drawn; many details require to be filled in, and no doubt many really important facts have been left out altogether because of our ignorance.

Let us turn back to the question of the ductility

of metals, and consider whether the presence of the electrons helps us here also. We now see our atoms as spheres, all of them charged with positive electricity and packed closely; and we may perhaps be right in thinking that the electrons hold them together like a cement. But the most important point is that the atoms are not tied together by sharing electrons as in the diamond: they must rather repel each other than otherwise, being all charged with positive electricity. They are free to roll or slide over each other, because they are not attached to each other at definite points, as often occurs in other crystals. These things seem helpful when we consider the slipping of one plane over another.

So far we have been considering the crystalline structure and properties of a few of the metals in the pure state. Now in practice we meet with alloys far more often than with pure metals, and that for the reason that alloys have properties of their own of the greatest value. Alloys are, in fact, extraordinarily interesting in their immense variety and in the wide range of their usefulness. New forms are constantly being discovered. No matter what peculiar virtue may be required for some special purpose, an alloy of some sort is forthcoming which satisfies the demand more or

THE NATURE OF CRYSTALS

less completely. We must try to see some reason for these things, if we can, in what we have recently discovered. Of course, we know so little as yet, and there is so much to explain, that in a few years' time we may think very little of our present attempts, but we must make a beginning.

It very often happens that the addition to a metal of quite a small quantity of a second metal, or even a non-metal, causes a notable improvement in hardness. Pure metals are generally very soft, because their slip planes are so ready to give. The first of all the great alloys was bronze, a mixture of copper and tin, which is far harder than either metal alone. The mixture of copper and zinc produces the serviceable brass, of which there are varying qualities, depending on the proportions of the mixture. Steel is formed by the addition of a small percentage of carbon to pure iron. There are alloys of copper and aluminium, which are very tough and do not corrode, but are difficult to work in the shaping machine. There is an alloy of copper and nickel, which does not corrode and is easily moulded; it is used for the coverings of bullets. German silver is a white, ductile alloy, non-corroding, which is used in the manufacture of such articles as spoons and forks, which are afterwards coated with silver in the process known as electroplating. An alloy of nickel with chromium stands very great heat, and is used for the wiring of electric furnaces. Chromium, cobalt and tungsten combined in definite proportions make stellite, an extraordinarily hard, non-corroding substance; some of the standard weights at the National Physical Laboratory are being made of it. There are alloys for the making of bells, very soft alloys for type metal, and a great variety of solders. There is the aluminium bronze, which is used for cheap jewellery and consists of aluminium with a small percentage of copper. And so on to a long list, if it were necessary to make one.

Let us take one of the simpler cases—for example, that in which the addition of a small quantity of aluminium to copper produces an increase in hardness. The X-rays show that the structure of the copper crystals remains the same, except that here and there an aluminium atom takes the place of a copper atom. Now the weakness of the crystal lies, as we have seen, in the fact that one part slides on another part along a certain plane. This plane is now no longer even: there is a scattering of aluminium atoms in it, and we can readily suppose that the

THE NATURE OF CRYSTALS

slipping has become more difficult, and that we have here the cause of hardening.[1] There is a remarkable effect which makes us think we are right in supposing so. The atoms of aluminium must strain the structure of the copper crystal, because the copper will not take up more than a certain number. If an alloy is made containing more than about 10 per cent. of aluminium, the X-rays tell us that the copper crystals are broken up altogether, and a new structure is formed.[2] The aluminium atoms must be distorting the copper crystal, and this fits in very well with the fact that it hardens the copper. On the other hand, when nickel is added to copper the atoms of the former replace the atoms of the latter to any extent: evidently they can slip into the places of the copper atoms without straining the copper crystals at all. And in this case there is no hardening effect, which is just what we should expect. It is only when we push in atoms which really strain the copper crystal and make its planes uneven that the hardening is brought about. We have jammed the sliding planes.

[1] Rosenhain, "The Inner Structure of Alloys," Institute of Metals, May 2, 1923.
[2] Jette, Phragmen and Westgren, Institute of Metals, March 1921.

In the case of steel the action is of the same kind, but here the carbon atoms that are the cause of the hardening do not replace the iron atoms, but are forced into the empty spaces between them. We can easily see that this may distort the iron crystal, and as before prevent the movement along a plane of slip. Once again there is a limit to the amount of the alloying substance: only a small percentage of carbon can be introduced into the iron without breaking up its ordinary simple structure.

The problems of iron and steel contain, however, many more complications than this. We have only to ask what happens when more carbon is put in than the iron structure can carry, and we find we have a new problem. Amongst other things, a new crystal appears, formed of molecules, each containing three atoms of iron and one of carbon; it is known as cementite. The new crystals are very hard and unyielding, and in form are like needles (Plate XXVIII). Their presence hardens the iron very greatly and makes it difficult to work. A beautiful example of its effect on steel is to be found in the old swords that once made their way from India through Damascus into Europe. Damascus steel was greatly valued for the excellence of its qualities. Fine specimens

PLATE XXVII.

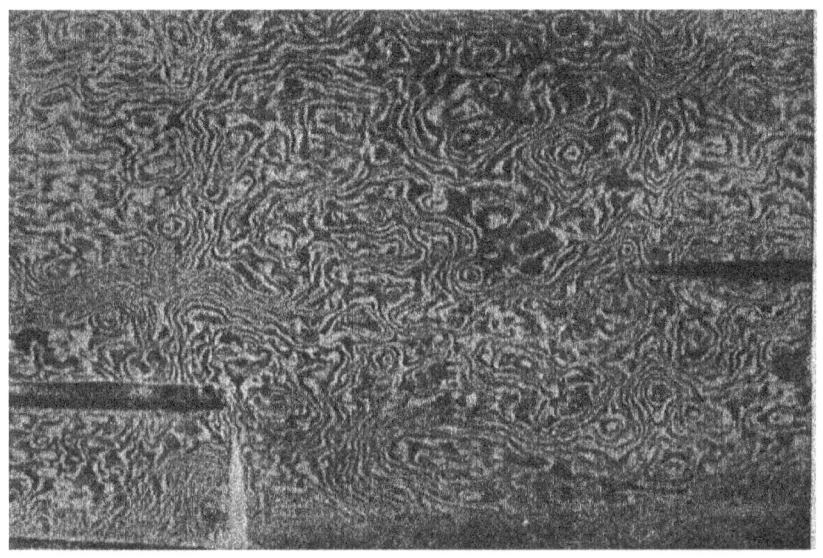

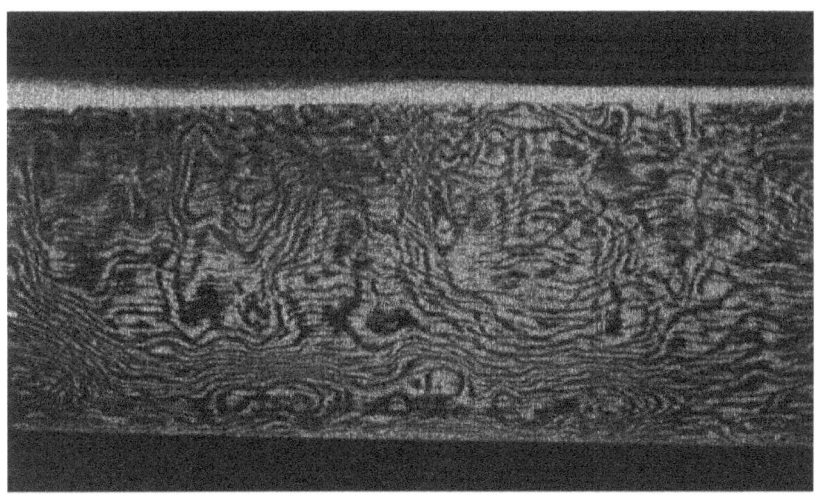

[*By courtesy of the University of London Press, Ltd.*
Damascus blades.
(From Belaiew's "Crystallisation of Metals.")

PLATE XXVIII.

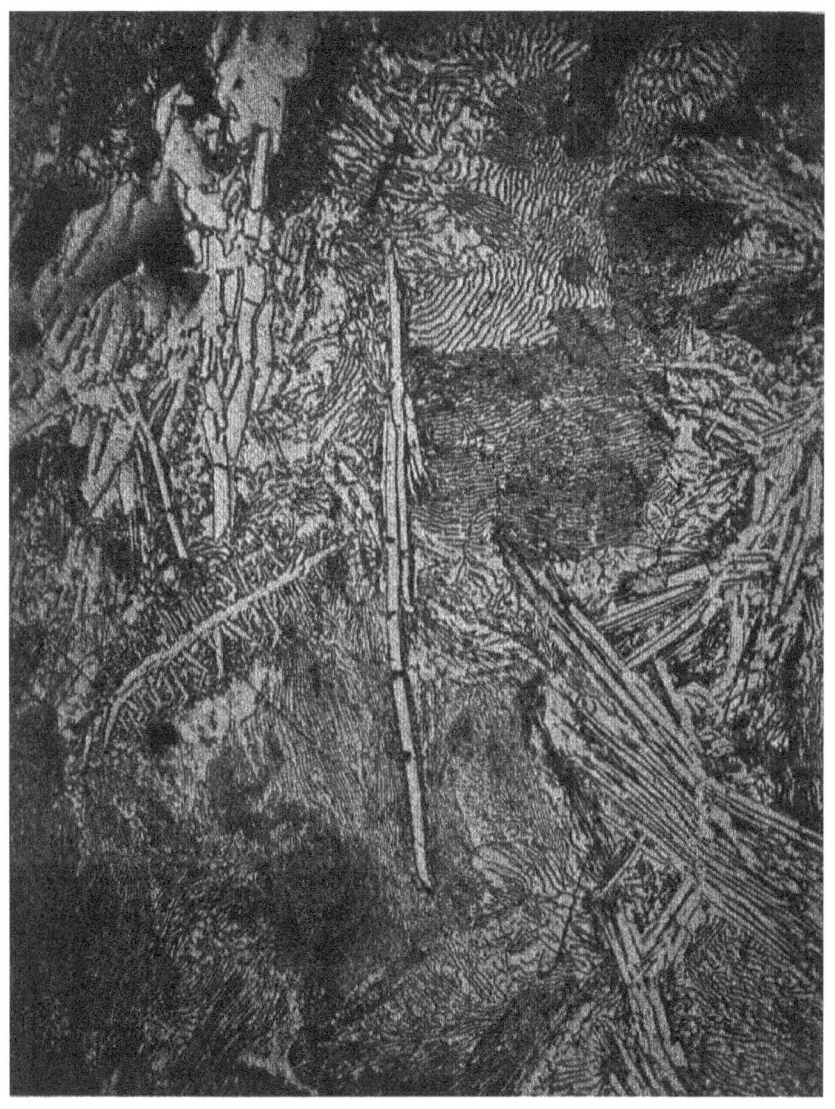

[By courtesy of the University of London Press, Ltd.

The long needle-shaped bodies are cementite crystals forming part of the general mass of steel.
(From Belaiew's "Crystallisation of Metals.)

THE NATURE OF CRYSTALS

are to be seen in the Wallace Collection; they show the characteristic wavy pattern (Plate XXVII) which has always been looked on as evidence of genuineness. When examined under the microscope the lines of the pattern are seen to consist of multitudes of dots, forming a sort of milky way in the steel. These dots are the tiny crystals of cementite. As Colonel Belaiew tells us, the steel when it was first made was most difficult to work. The smith, with his little furnace, would heat the steel red hot, but after he had struck but a few blows and made a slight impression on the steel, the momentary softening had gone. The hardness due to the cementite crystals had only been removed for an instant. More heating, a few more blows and slowly the steel became less rigid. In fact, the cementite crystals were changing their form. They were becoming less like needles, gathering themselves together into more rounded shapes, and as they did so the steel became more pliable (Plate XXIX A). At last the fine Damascus steel was reached, so strong and yet so elastic. It is very likely that much of the keen edge that these swords would take was due to the presence of the very hard particles embodied and held in the softer iron. The edge would be like a saw with extremely fine teeth. In the trial of skill between Saladin and King Richard which Walter Scott describes in "The Talisman," the former threw a gossamer veil into the air and severed it by drawing his scimitar across it, a fine test of keenness and of skill. Richard, on the other hand, used his sword like an axe, and clove in two an iron bar, the mace of one of his knights. This also was a test requiring great qualities in the steel, but on the part of the man the skill lay more in the power to strike a terrific blow than in delicacy of touch.

Grinding, sharpening and polishing are really very interesting operations. When we put a knife on the grindstone we let the hard crystals in the stone cut minute furrows in the steel, actually removing the material. This is one stage of the sharpening process. But the polishing on the oil-stone or the strop is a different thing altogether. Here we actually make the steel to flow, smoothing down the furrow; sometimes, as Sir George Beilby has shown, actually drawing a skin of metal over the deeper hollows. The metal seems to remain crystalline all the time; the X-rays show readily the crystals in a razor blade. Probably the action is the same as that which took place in the gold leaves when they were heated. The oil that we use helps in the

PLATE XXIX.

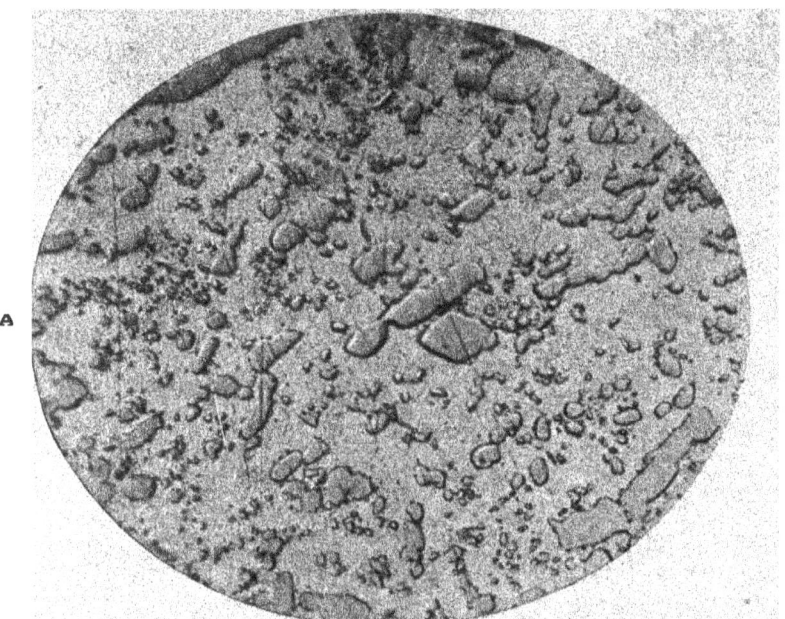

[*By courtesy of the University of London Press, Ltd.*

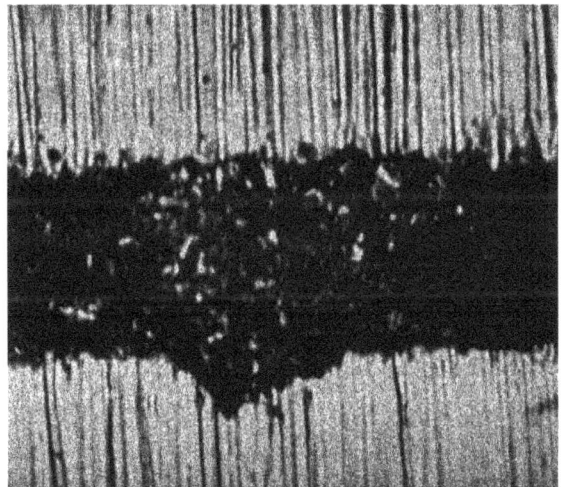

[*By courtesy of Sir George Beilby.*

A. Section magnified a thousand times and showing the cementite needles in process of being broken up and rounded off.
    (From Belaiew's "Crystallisation of Metals.")
B. The dark band is a scratch made by a very fine needle in a polished piece of speculum (mirror) metal, highly magnified. The fine vertical scratches are made by emery powder in polishing. Many small particles have been torn up and deposited in the trough made by the needle.
    (From Beilby's "Aggregation and Flow of Solids.")

PLATE XXX.

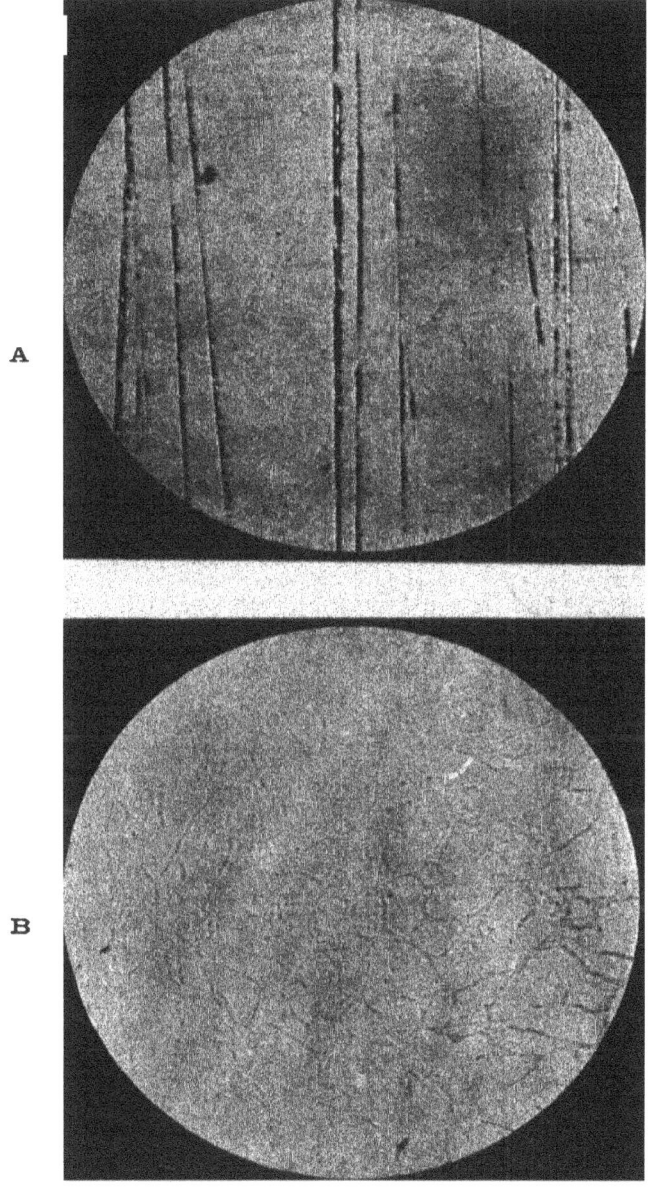

In A a piece of speculum metal, after being rubbed with fine emery, has been polished with rouged leather. The metal has been dragged over the emery scratches; there is a reminiscence of butter spread on bread. In B the polishing with rouge has been carried further; the emery scratches have disappeared, but the outlines of the grains in the metal begin to appear.
(From Sir George Beilby's "**Aggregation and Flow of Solids**," by courtesy of the author.)

THE NATURE OF CRYSTALS

smoothing process. The metal is strained by the flow; in time the strain tends to come undone, and heat especially can take away the keenness of the edge (Plates XXIX B, XXX, XXXI).

An alloy is generally a much worse conductor of electricity than a pure metal. It may well be that when the stranger atoms are forced into the structure of the pure metal, and the planes of atoms are made uneven, the electrons are more hampered in their passage through the metal. More energy is required to force them along, and the metal becomes hotter through the passage of the current than if it were pure. In the case of a pure metal, as I have already said, the resistance to the movement of the electrons becomes greater if the temperature is raised. We can imagine that the electrons find it harder to get past the atoms when the latter are more active; heat makes them move to and fro more quickly about their proper positions. But heat does not make so much difference in the case of alloys, because the passage of the electrons is already so difficult that heat does not make much change. We can show this by a simple experiment :—

A battery sends a current round a circuit which has two branches as in the figure (Plate XXXII A). One of them contains a coil of copper wire M, and a lamp L_1, the other a coil of an alloy such as German silver, for example, and a lamp L_2. The coils are so adjusted in respect to the resistance which they offer to the passage of the electric current through them that the lamps both burn dimly. A vessel containing liquid air is brought up so as to include the coil M, and the lamp L_1 at once burns brightly. The cooling of the copper wire has lowered its resistance to the passage of electrons, and more current flows through the lamp. But when the alloy is, in its turn, immersed in liquid air, no change is made.

Sometimes metals crystallise in more than one way. Iron furnishes one of the simplest and most striking examples. At ordinary temperatures the iron atoms are arranged so that each atom has eight neighbours. The latter are at the corners of a tiny cube, of which the former atom occupies the centre. This is not the closest form of packing, as will readily be found on trial. The packing of the pile of shot of which I spoke before gives the closest packing, and in that each shot has twelve neighbours, six touching it round an equator, and three more round a line of latitude in each hemisphere: or, as we may put it, six in its own layer and three in each of the next layers. It is the packing of gold, silver, copper

PLATE XXXI.

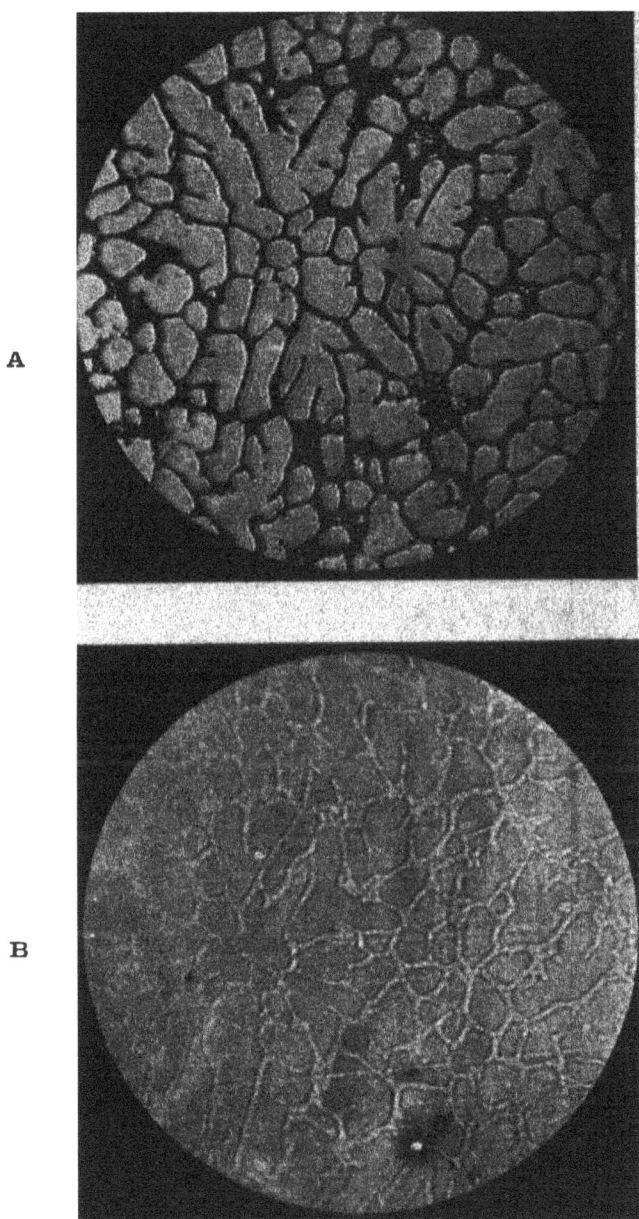

A

B

In A the metal has been etched with acid; the "flowed" parts have been readily attacked and removed, the grains now show up very clearly. In B polishing has begun again.

(From Sir George Beilby's "Aggregation and Flow of Solids," by courtesy of the author.)

PLATE XXXII.

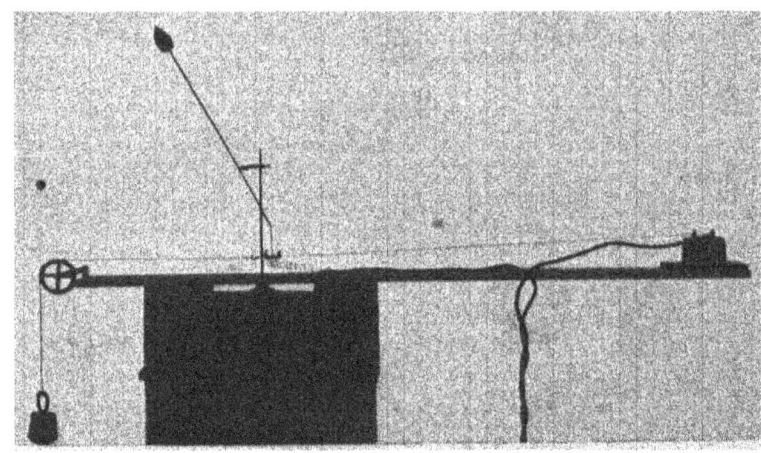

A. The resistance of the pure metal coil in the same circuit as the shining lamp has been reduced by surrounding it with a freezing mixture.
B. The iron wire is stretched by a hanging weight; its expansion and contraction are magnified by the lever arrangement. The wire is heated by passing an electric current along it.

THE NATURE OF CRYSTALS

and aluminium. It is very curious that when iron is heated to a cherry red the atoms change their arrangement and pack in the tightest form, that of the pile of shot. The effect is easiest to see when an iron wire is heated beyond this point and allowed to cool. When it comes to the critical temperature, the atoms suddenly adopt the looser packing and the wire stretches a little : the increase of length is easily observed by the use of some magnifying device. It is very curious, too, that when the old form changes to the new, some energy is set free and the iron suddenly brightens up again. The stretching and brightening have long been matters of observation, but it is only quite recently that we have discovered that the packing of the atoms into two different crystalline forms is at the bottom of what we have seen (Plate XXXII B).

These very few instances of the relation between the properties of a metal and its crystal structure are drawn from an immense subject, most of it still waiting exploration with our new helpers, the X-rays. We cannot say beforehand what will be found out. We can be very sure, however, that the better we understand our materials the better use we can make of them.

NOTE

AFTER trials of many ways of making models of atomic structure and of many substances I find that two have real merits :—

Balls representing the atoms may be made of hard dentists' wax, which softens in boiling water and can then be pressed into proper shape in metal moulds made for the purpose, just as we used to remake our golf-balls in the old days. The spherical mould is made in two halves; and it is convenient to mount them in the lathe, one on the head and one on the back centre. Small balls harden at once, and can be made very quickly: larger balls must be left a little while in the mould. The hard wax can be drilled without becoming softened and deformed by the heat generated in drilling. The models made of the wax are very finished in appearance, and will stand all ordinary temperatures. The wax is rather costly.

Wooden balls can be obtained much more cheaply than wax. I have bought them from Messrs. Maxime, Ltd., 6 Featherstone St., City Road, E.C. 2. They can only be obtained in certain sizes, but these are reasonably convenient: moreover, they are not so truly spherical as the wax balls. But they are good enough for practical purposes.

Gramophone needles made good connectors: the balls, wax or wood, being drilled to receive them. The holes should be drilled true and in correct position. Convenient little contrivances can be made to be used for this purpose on the lathe.

www.ingramcontent.com/pod-product-compliance
Lightning Source LLC
Chambersburg PA
CBHW031707230426
43668CB00006B/134